T0285179

MY FATHER'S BURNING IN HELL

a memoir

MIA MCDANIEL

RARE BIRD
LOS ANGELES, CALIFORNIA

RARE BIRD

Tʜɪs ɪs ᴀ Gᴇɴᴜɪɴᴇ Rᴀʀᴇ Bɪʀᴅ Bᴏᴏᴋ

Rare Bird Books
6044 North Figueroa Street
Los Angeles, CA 90042
rarebirdbooks.com

For more information, address:
Rare Bird Books Subsidiary Rights Department
6044 North Figueroa Street
Los Angeles, CA 90042

Set in Minion
Printed in the United States

10 9 8 7 6 5 4 3 2 1

Publisher's Cataloging-in-Publication Data available upon request.

Richard, my wonderful, amazing, good-looking husband
who always protects me.

Bake and Steeckala, you two are the best ever and continue
to make my life wonderful.

Simon, my hip and trendy brother for his chutzpah,
and for living that life with me.

And for Anna, the bravest woman I have ever known,
who prevailed over alarming adversity.

Contents

Prologue

My father was a narcissist. Not your run-of-the-mill braggart, superiority complex alpha male. But one who could make Donald Trump blush. He was charming, sweet, and loving when it suited him. He was mean-spirited and manipulative when it didn't. And I longed for his flawed love more than anything—as a child, a teen, a single woman, a married woman, and a mother.

Born in 1930 to Polish Jews who immigrated to New York City via Ellis Island, he was a middle child with a brother twelve years older and a sister ten years younger. His childhood was unhappy. He had a sweet, loving mother who didn't read or write English, and a brutish father who didn't break up fights with his brother and ignored him when he was mean to his little sister.

All that makes me wonder: Is his behavior as a young adult, a married man, a father acceptable because of his difficult upbringing? Because he had a particularly rough childhood, is he excused from societal and familial norms? Is a bad childhood a legitimate excuse for bad behavior the rest of his life?

And when you reach a certain age—thirty-five, forty, forty-five— is it time to forgive your parents and move past your bad childhood?

This is my story.

Chapter 1

Anna

I never told my children that I had a cousin named Anna. My then-husband, Rob, knew of her, but they'd never met. And until a few weeks earlier, I hadn't seen her for nearly thirty-two years. It was 2005.

Anna had lived in Calabasas, located on the Westside of the San Fernando Valley in Southern California, for more than twenty years with her third husband, Bruce, a decent, hard-working, handsome man, and her daughter, Linda, from her second husband. They had a lovely townhome with a beautiful yard filled with flowers, plants, umbrellas, and chaise lounges that they shared with their two cats and a dog. A small three-bedroom home, it was lovingly decorated with warm, comfortable furniture, Thomas Kinkade paintings, Lladró sculptures, and family photos. One of the bedrooms had her sewing machine, reminding her of the aunt she lived with in New York when she first arrived in America.

Living in the same community was Anna's stepfather, George, who had been a part of her life since she was fourteen. Her dear, sweet mother passed away in 2003. Anna and George loved each other and genuinely liked each other. He was nearly ninety-three, so she took him shopping and to doctor's appointments and especially loved to bring him his favorite home-cooked meals, including chicken soup and brisket and baked goods like rugelach and cherry pie. He, in turn, tried and rarely succeeded in giving her "pocket money." Life was good after many difficult, tumultuous years. Anna was an ultrasound technician and regularly volunteered at the local thrift shop that benefitted the Jewish Community Foundation in Los Angeles. She was excited and nervous at the prospect of seeing me for just the second time in thirty-five years and meeting my children, Samantha (Sam, twenty), and Michael (seventeen), and my husband for the first time.

It was a Saturday afternoon when she drove the forty minutes to our family's home on Mulholland Drive in Bel Air. A bittersweet irony, as Anna had honestly considered driving off the steep, windy, cliffside road when she'd been abandoned by her first husband in 1972.

Sam and Michael were excited and a little anxious to meet her. They were curious as to why I had never told them about Anna before, especially since she lived so close to us. It was very complicated, and I wanted them to be a little older when they finally met. Growing up, I didn't know anyone with a family history resembling mine in the slightest. I just didn't want my children to know of the trauma and chaos their mother experienced until I felt they might be ready.

Anna trembled as she walked up the winding stairs to the front door. You could see the San Fernando Valley and the mountains in the reflection of the giant floor-to-ceiling windows in the living room. It was a beautiful two-story home with four bedrooms, an open-concept great room, and a unique black-and-white chandelier—a reproduction of one on display at MOMA—hanging over the white lacquer table and chairs in the dining room. The backyard was angled up to the home directly above ours. It was a bit mountainous, and there was plenty of space between our neighbors on the famed street. The view was exquisite, particularly in the cooler months when the wind made the smog less visible. There was a large deck off the kitchen door, adorned with flowers, plants, and a hot tub. Depending on the season, the deck would have American flags on the Fourth, pumpkins and witches on Halloween, or Chanukah decorations and Christmas lights in December. Inside were our two cats (indoor

Mia McDaniel

cats because of the coyotes) and our adored long-haired chihuahua, Mick, who became Sir Mick when Mick Jagger was knighted.

We had recently renovated the kitchen, and it was stunning: Viking appliances, blond hardwood floors, blue and white cabinets, and white marbled granite countertops. Wonderful artwork adorned our walls: Andy Warhol, Erté, Al Hirschfeld. Lots and lots of books. An extensive collection of books authored by my very favorite, Joyce Carol Oates. All of Oscar Hijuelos' books. Joan Didion. A. M. Homes. Steve Martin, for fun. There were more than a hundred poetry books, as Rob was a poet when he wasn't a full-time advertising executive. The first poem he wrote was "So Six" that was about our daughter Sam when she was six. I always thought it was the sweetest, most endearing poem he'd ever written.

Fresh flowers were always on the dining room table. Big white hydrangeas or tall red lilies.

In the side yard, our little hamster was buried in his handmade coffin, along with the goldfish that died. And on the concrete was a basketball hoop. What the kids loved best about our backyard was that its design was perfect for a game of "Capture the Flag." Friends' backyards were envied for their space or swimming pools, but they couldn't compare to Sam and Michael's backyard for their favorite outdoor game.

In the front yard, the gardener tended to gorgeous flowers and plants and three bonsai trees that were carefully pruned. And there was a hummingbird feeder that attracted the stunning birds—and sometimes the ants on the ground.

It was disproportionately important for me to impress Anna with my home. With my children. With my husband. With our possessions. After all, Anna only knew me as an insecure young girl she cared for when she was just a child herself. I desperately wanted to make a stellar impression.

Chapter 2
Mia

I was born on the Lower East Side of Manhattan in November 1953 to Rosemarie (Rose) and Arthur Weinberg, twelve months after they married. My mother was eighteen; my father was twenty-two. The attraction was immediate. Rose was a petite 5'1" beauty with long, dark hair, and Arthur at 5'11" was tall, dark, and handsome. They both saw marriage as a way to escape their families. They struggled to make it work, but the foundation was already cracked with two immature, insecure, and selfish young adults.

My father did everything he could to support his young wife and baby. He drove a city cab; he bartended; he sold LPs and 45s at the local record store. All this while attending college at night. We lived in a meager apartment, but my mother made it look pretty with flowers, plants, and needlepoint pillows. And there were always bright, colorful dish towels and potholders.

My parents told me I was a sweet little girl with lots of freckles and personality. I was a good sleeper. And I was easily entertained. The big Quaker Oats oatmeal container with the bright red and blue Quaker kept me happy for hours, putting small toys into it and taking the same small toys out of it. I squealed with delight every night when my daddy came home. I was three when I got my first cat and ever since then I've had two or three cats, so no beast would be lonely. And a dog, too.

I roller-skated New York City streets before I walked. My mother and I sailed down the streets with skate key in hand, lest she had to adjust them. Our little family of three struggled but was content for the first few years, and my parents were convinced they had the most beautiful, intelligent, precious, wonderful child in the whole wide world. They seemed to adore me.

And when I was four and a half, my baby brother, Simon, was born.

Chapter 3
Samantha & Frederick

My grandparents, Samantha and Frederick, immigrated to New York City from Germany in 1938. Moving to the United States required a sponsor to agree to provide housing until the refugees could provide for themselves. Frederick had cousins in New York who sponsored him, and family legend has it that he boarded an enormous ship to Ellis Island with eight dollars in his pocket and few possessions. He spent nine months with his cousins and saved enough money to send for my grandmother and my mother.

They came to the United States from a little town near Hamburg where they lived in a sweet, very small apartment. In 1938, when my mother was nearly four, their lives were becoming increasingly scary and dangerous. The Nazis were coming to their neighborhood, as well as marching across the entire country, and upper-middle class Jews were warned to flee Germany because of the impending invasion. Frederick was a "glazier"; he owned a glassmaking store. He was duly warned, and they began to make arrangements to leave their homeland. Then, his store was destroyed. Along with death and destruction, unimaginable atrocities were taking place throughout the country and in neighboring countries. There were concentration camps. The Holocaust. Relatives and friends of everyone, including my family, who did not escape, perished.

They initially found a tiny, old apartment in Brooklyn that desperately needed repairs. But after nine long months of separation, they were so thrilled to be together again, it might as well have been Buckingham Palace.

In 1946, when my mother was twelve, my grandparents had enough savings to put a down payment on a beautiful, small home in Riverdale, New York. It had two bedrooms, one that was fondly called "the little room" because it was so tiny. It was my oma's sewing room (that Anna fondly recalled her whole life). The living room was, to a little girl like me, so elegant. It had a very modern couch with brown and beige curves that looked like a big "S" and stood on what was considered luxurious beige wall-to-wall carpeting. This couch would be where Anna made her bed every evening and put her linens and pillow away every morning. She had her clothes in a small dresser in "the little room" with Oma's sewing machine. She had a tiny portion of the closet in the home's entrance, where winter coats, scarves, and hats were hung, as well as the few dresses and blouses she had. And to put away her shoes and one pair of boots.

There was a small kitchen where Oma was always cooking or baking something fabulous, including brisket, giant and puffy matzo balls—not prepared with the box mix—and rhubarb pies. She taught Anna how to make all of it. Anna was very attentive when Aunt Samantha baked her pies. Years later she baked her own using her aunt's recipes.

There was checkered black-and-white linoleum and an enormous, black rotary phone attached to the kitchen wall. And they had two sets of dishes because Oma kept kosher. I do remember when I was in my teens that Opa had his own "bacon pan."

The master bedroom had a beautiful off-white chenille bedspread with pink, green, and yellow flowers. And matching pillows. A large Lane dresser with six enormous drawers. Two nightstands, each hiding a delicious German chocolate bar. When Simon and I were old enough to sleep over, Oma and Opa carried us to their bed and gave us each a big square of the chocolate bar. When our grandparents were ready for bed, they carried us into the living room and laid us on the beautiful sofa, with the dining room chairs strategically placed around it so we wouldn't fall. It was so sweet. So kind. So unnecessary. If we had fallen onto the soft carpeting from a sofa that was only a few feet high, it's unlikely we would have been injured. Simon and I adored our grandparents.

The house also had a one-bedroom apartment upstairs with a separate entrance. They rented it out, and the income helped pay their mortgage.

On the ground floor, beneath the steps to the front door, was the basement that Opa converted into his carpentry shop after teaching himself how to create and build custom cabinets. He was a cabinetmaker until he retired and moved to Miami Beach with Oma more than twenty years later.

I especially loved the little cabinetry shop and spent most of the day playing with the bowls, glasses, plates, and silverware that Opa had stored for me there. I had so much fun making sawdust pies and cakes near the enormous saw, which Opa always made sure was unplugged and safe. I saw the beautiful, scantily clad ladies in the Vargas pin-up calendar by the front door. I assumed Opa thought I was either too young or too short to notice it.

The backyard was so much fun, even though it needed mowing or weeding most of the time. My brother and I played with pails and shovels and watered the grass. And we loved playing with our grandparent's pet boxers: mother Betty and her daughter Donna. Two years later, we would take Betty home to be our dog.

An enormous cherry tree sprawled above the carport where Opa and Simon and I picked cherries. After we picked a small bowlful, he helped us down. He got the ladder and went back up to harvest enough cherries for Oma to bake a cherry pie. Oma was my favorite person in the whole world from the time I was about eight.

"My oma was everything to me. She was always there. I adored her from when I was really little. And, as an adult, she became the most important and cherished woman in my life. I leaned on her all the time. Because she could take it. My parents were virtually absent, even when they were present. I'm sure I wouldn't be this happy today if not for my oma," I told Anna when we were both living in Southern California in the mid-2000s.

Opa kept his legendary car parked in the carport. He drove a 1960 dark purple Ford Galaxie 500. He was way ahead of his time when he glued a black plastic phone receiver, complete with a coiled cord, onto his dashboard. This way he could deliver his cabinets to his customers in New York and New Jersey while appearing to be "making calls and answering the phone." Other drivers and passengers were astonished watching him "on his phone." This was in the early sixties; no one could believe their eyes.

Simon and I met Anna for the first time at Oma and Opa's house. It was 1958; I was almost five. We had a wonderful dinner that Oma and Anna prepared—chicken soup with matzo balls, brisket, tzimmes (sweetened carrots), challah, and a delicious mouth-watering cherry pie. I remember it so well. It was a beautiful, delicious, and very loving meal.

Growing up, I understood that my grandparents adored my mother. They provided for her for most of her life, during the difficult years when she and my dad were struggling and before, during, and after two of my mother's three divorces. Had they been alive when she divorced her third husband, they undoubtedly would have assisted her then too.

Chapter 4

Anna

Anna had a dismal childhood. Her father, David, was the youngest of my grandmother's three brothers. David's brothers didn't escape the Nazis and were murdered in concentration camps. He and his wife, Irene, and daughter, Anna, lived in Gdańsk, Poland, for ten years and intended to move to Israel. The morning of their move, Irene, Anna, and David boarded their ship to Haifa. They talked; they rested; they ate breakfast. In the afternoon, they strolled the ship's decks and then sat down to lunch. By nightfall, their whole world had changed. David was dead. He had jumped overboard. A schizophrenic, David was convinced that Nazis were after him on the ship and jumping overboard was the only way to protect his family.

It was devastating. Horrifying. Unimaginable. Their beloved father/husband was dead. They were a family of three no longer. Irene and Anna were alone when the ship docked in Haifa, and Irene was forced to find work very quickly. She did so as a seamstress. But within weeks, she collapsed from exhaustion. She couldn't work and be there for Anna, so she found an orphanage, one that promised to return her when she could provide. They were heartbroken and apart for one year.

Their "forever goal" was to immigrate to the United States. In 1957, eleven-year-old Anna had the proper documentation and was within "the German quota" to enter the United States. At the time she was born, the town she lived in was considered Germany. For her mother, however, it was Poland, so she couldn't join her.

Anna flew to New York City on a giant propeller plane all by herself and was met by my maternal grandparents, Anna's aunt Samantha and uncle Frederick (my oma and opa) who she lived with. It would be two years before Anna would see her mother—having spent one year in the orphanage and then one year with her aunt and uncle. She enrolled in the sixth grade again and was held back because she could barely speak English. By the next year, she was nearly fluent and started eighth grade.

Life was strange for Anna, in a new country, with an aunt and uncle who were much older than her parents. But she felt safe. Stable. Though, not particularly happy.

Aunt Samantha was warm and loved Anna. She was good to her, but Anna regularly felt like she was treated more like a boarder than a niece or a daughter. Years later, I was distraught when she told me, "I never felt special or particularly cared about. I felt like I was a rescue from the pound." She knew her aunt was trying so hard to make Anna happy, but she also knew it was challenging for her aunt to be raising her brother's daughter when her own daughter was already in her twenties, married for five years with two children.

Uncle Frederick was not kind to her. He didn't care for Anna and told her she had an ugly face. "If I looked like you, I would keep my face in a toilet." Hurtful. Mean. Humiliating. And, as a beer-loving German, he thought Anna should learn to love it too. Every evening, he forced her to drink a beer with dinner. She despised the smell and taste of beer for the rest of her life. The family of three lived together for just over one year.

Chapter 5
Mia & Simon & Arthur & Rose

When Anna first moved in with her aunt and uncle, my family was preparing to move from our first house in Levittown, Long Island, where we'd lived for two years. It was a little 1,000 square foot house that my parents were able to afford because my grandparents gave them the down payment. It was so exciting to be in a real family neighborhood, so different from living in the city. Our development was nationally known as the nation's first mass-produced suburb.

About six months after we moved into our second home, which was a bit larger, my grandparents became increasingly concerned about Anna and talked with my parents frequently: "She's only twelve, and we're in our early fifties. It's too old for a little girl. And we live in the city. You're on Long Island where there are more families, and your new house has more room. Maybe Anna could move in with you?"

Not only was my immediate family much younger than my grandparents, but we were also upwardly mobile and my mother wanted to repay them for their care. Most importantly, she and my father knew it would be a much better lifestyle for Anna, so we invited her to join us in Plainview, a small town located on Long Island's north shore.

Our new house boasted a pretty front yard where my mother planted daises, roses, and geraniums. My father mowed the lawn and trimmed the hedges, and he barbequed on the weekends. It was the quintessential life in 1950s suburbia for our new family of five.

Mia McDaniel

When I learned that Anna would be living with us, I was absolutely thrilled. While Anna was my mother's cousin and Simon's and my second cousin, we embraced her from the very beginning. I was not even five and not only had a little brother whom I adored, but I would also now have an older sister. I was excited to tell everyone I knew and everyone I ever met about Anna, my new sister, who was of course *technically* my cousin.

Anna was happy about the move but very apprehensive. "I'm relieved, but I'm so nervous. Is this really going to be better than staying with you?" she asked my aunt.

"Darling, I understand you're anxious. She's my daughter and her family is wonderful. I'm sure it will be better."

"But what if Rose and Arthur don't like having me around all the time? What if their little girl doesn't like me? What if I don't like them? But I guess that wouldn't really matter. What if they're embarrassed by me? My accent? My looks? What if after two weeks, two months, two years, they change their minds? Who would take care of me then?"

"Anna, my sweetheart, let's give it a chance. They're happy to have you move in with them."

I was in the second grade, and Anna was in eighth grade. My mother was a homemaker, and my father had a new position as an engineer with an aircraft company. Still attending college, he would take nearly eleven years to graduate, while working, studying, and raising his family (however minimally).

It looked like Anna had little to worry about. The beautiful experiment with no evident downside enriched the family of four. She moved into the house in Plainview in 1959, about five months before her thirteenth birthday.

Finally, Anna thought she might be part of "a more normal family," as at twelve, she had already suffered devastating life experiences.

Chapter 6
Anna & Arthur

Anna was beginning to settle into her new home with the four of us. She was desperately trying to fit in and behave as the oldest child when my father began to notice her presence more and more. In short order, he became very attentive to her. Overly attentive. He was not a patient man; he had little patience for my mother or me and Simon. But he had plenty of patience for Anna. It started with homework. He helped her in math and science. It became an evening ritual. And she started getting more A's. He was very affectionate— "lovely dovey" she called it years later.

Shortly after Anna went to bed, my father would come into her bedroom at night, after watching television downstairs with my mother. They talked about her day. He was warm and sweet, and he would give her a goodnight kiss. On the forehead. On the cheek. On the mouth. Then wherever he could convince her was okay. She became his prey. He told her that everything they did was about love. It was right. Even appropriate. He loved her, and he was simply showing her. She thought nothing of it. She thought it was normal because he told her so. She was his blank slate at almost thirteen years old.

He wanted more. He touched. He kissed. He sucked. He licked. And then, he penetrated. She missed her period the second time they had sex. He told her to take a warm bath, adding, "If that doesn't work, I'll send you to Sweden to get an abortion."

What a compassionate man. She was lucky, however, when the blood flowed heavily the next month. He wanted more "affection," as he called it, and he wanted it regularly. He insisted she see a doctor for a prescription for the new birth control pill, and he made an appointment for her. She took the subway by herself to the city and found the physician's office. She told the doctor what my father told her to say—"I have such terrible cramps when I get my period, I need a prescription for the pill." It was a lie, but now they wouldn't have to worry about a pregnancy.

She felt loved for the first time in her life by someone besides her mother and father. Arthur had never been a father figure to her. He was Dad to me and to Simon, but not to her. She was the cousin who lived with us. And, over and over again, he told her their relationship was all good. All loving. The patriarch of the family, who had taken her in to love her, help her assimilate, and eventually put down roots, abused her. And lied to her. And took advantage of her. And told her that she shouldn't tell anyone because it was their "'beautiful, loving secret."

Chapter 7

Anna

After a very short time living with my family, Anna had household chores, such as setting the table and cleaning up after dinner. She often took care of me and Simon. I thought it was just perfect. My older sister was now part of the family. Anna, though, didn't feel like the welcomed older sister but more like the live-in babysitter and housecleaner. Despite all of this, she still believed that Arthur loved her the most. After all, he couldn't possibly show another the affection and love he showed her on his nighttime visits, not even his wife.

My mother, who could be a particularly warm woman, was not warm to Anna. She seemed incapable of embracing Anna in the way Anna had hoped. The "three kids," however, loved each other's company.

In 1959, Anna's mother immigrated to the United States, and the following year she married her second husband, George. He was very kind to Anna and Irene, and he remained special to Anna until he died in 2017. For twenty years, he drove a candy truck. It was literally a treat when they visited. He brought chocolates, sourballs, and nougats. While the two wished Anna could live with them, they were grateful to my family that she didn't have to stay in their small, uncomfortable apartment in the city.

Mia McDaniel

Chapter 8
Arthur & Anna & Rose

In the early sixties, my father's star was rising fast, and he took a new position at an engineering firm, this time heading up marketing and advertising. It was a huge promotion, and his salary was more than double what he had previously earned. It was time to move again. To a bigger, better, more beautiful new house—our fourth residence in less than five years (this would become a recurring theme for my family). The job was in Morris Plains, New Jersey, an affluent suburb in the north that served as a bedroom community for those working in New York. Our new house was a stunning 3,400 square foot split-level house with five bedrooms, an enormous chef's kitchen, and a family room. There was a huge living room that took up an entire floor with a gorgeous blue silk couch and a very expensive, very "state-of-the-art" stereo system built into a stunning maple cabinet. In the eye-popping, sunken dining room that sat off the living room on a lower level were an Italian provincial dining room table and six chairs that were likely the most extravagant furniture on the small block of stately homes. Atop the table was a magnificent black marble centerpiece in the shape of a serpent. The home and its furnishings were extraordinary. My mother had impeccable taste, and we could afford, for the first time, expensive pieces. The fifth bedroom was for Eula, our new live-in maid. There was a half-acre of forest behind the beautiful backyard. My mother created a stunning rock garden with nine different flowers and plants. The community pool was a short walk through the woods and Anna, Simon, and

I would swim there often in the summertime, sometimes joined by our parents. The house was on a cul-de-sac with only six houses on the entire block. To me, Simon, and Anna, it was a mansion. It was 1961. Anna was fourteen and a half years old.

She was growing into a pretty young girl. Not nearly as awkward or as uncomfortable as she had been when she first arrived in the US. She had long, thick dark hair, a pretty face (though it took her years to believe that after what my grandfather had said to her), and a good figure, which she was vigilant about keeping that way, as my father insisted. She was a quiet young girl, who kept to herself. She never wanted to cause any trouble. She never wanted to be asked to leave. And I knew nothing about what she was feeling or doing with my own father. I was a little girl of seven, with parents who cared more about themselves and their careers than my brother and me, while my father was more interested in Anna.

Anna was doing very well in school, ever since my father started working with her. She always worked very hard and spent more time on homework than other kids. She was shy and terribly insecure about her accent. And her clothes and her hairdo, none of which she thought were right. She never felt pretty. It was all so overwhelming. At least on the weekends, it started to be more fun, as she made girlfriends and they took the bus to "super stores" like Walmart, where she used the silver dollars Aunt Samantha had given her to buy fancy, frilly blouses and wonderful costume jewelry.

It was commonplace for my mother, who was a wonderful cook, to prepare delicious family meals a few times a week in the luxurious dining room. On a night I have long remembered and found so very sad, we were eating beef stroganoff. Anna forked a mushroom soaking in gravy. She inspected it closely and proceeded to smell it. She had never seen a mushroom before. Upon seeing her sniffing the vegetable, my mother nearly shrieked, "Anna. What on earth are you doing? You don't smell your food, you silly girl. You eat it like a normal person. What were you thinking? You can't be that stupid." My father

Mia McDaniel

laughed loudly in response. In spite of their secret relationship, my father joined my mother in mocking Anna. Anna was humiliated. She turned a deep pink and sat rigidly with us for the duration of the meal. Eating quietly. Not speaking. The only lesson I learned that evening was not to smell my food. Maybe in the recesses of my little mind, I also learned to be kind to your children. Not to ever shame them. It was one incident of a seemingly never-ending campaign of mockery, degradation, and emotional and sexual abuse for Anna.

It's still a mystery to me why my mother was particularly unkind to Anna, but I suspect it was because of her insecurities. She spent a lot of her time trying to be attractive and youthful, and I think she was worried that as Anna got older, she might look prettier than her. I think this concerned my mother, not necessarily with respect to just my father, but her world in general. She wanted to be the most captivating woman in her house.

As far as Anna's abuse by my father, I think my mother must have been aware of their depraved relationship but unable to fully process it. She chose to ignore it instead and take advantage of Anna, causing her to feel that she was nothing more than "the help," rather than a member of our family. While my father was clearly molesting and carefully grooming my young cousin to become the woman and sexual partner he wanted, my mother was relying on Anna more and more. For babysitting. For housekeeping. For whatever tasks she didn't feel like doing for our family. Anna felt less like a member of the family than ever before. Except for the nights alone with my father. She became an unpaid babysitter, a housekeeper (even though we had a live-in maid), and an errand girl, when she was old enough to drive. My mother wanted to be a professional woman. My father wanted her to be a housewife and mother. At that time, we really didn't need the money. Nevertheless, my mother got a job in the city as a knitwear consultant to Arnold Constable, a department store that catered to the rich and elite. She thrived as Anna suffered. Anna was required to spend even more time watching us, as if she was an au pair (though Anna told me in 2007 that she believed she would have been treated far better if she were an au pair). Now both my parents worked all day. After school in the late afternoon when Anna got home, she took over from Eula and made me snacks and played games with me. She watched my baby brother, and on occasion, was asked to start dinner when my mother was running late.

My dad was now a full-fledged executive, and my parents were hosting extravagant dinner parties. Anna was often called upon to help my mother with the preparation and serving, though, of course, neither Anna nor my little brother and I were ever welcome to dine with my parents at these gatherings. We were, however, brought out in fancy clothes to be "oohed" and "aahed" at, before eating dinner in our bedrooms. While my mother prepared wonderful menus, she also made sure to wear whatever dress my father liked best to show off her sexy figure to all the guests, particularly the males (and her clothing was primarily elegant designer labels that hugged her beautiful shape). Between the preparation and dressing, she was usually a nervous wreck, and it was Anna who bore the brunt of her anxiety.

In our large new house, we each had our own bedroom. Mine was designed with a cat motif, and had a matching bedspread, curtains, and pillows on a plush white carpet, while Simon's was about sports, with a bedspread full of footballs, baseballs, and basketballs, matching curtains and the same white wall-to-wall carpeting. This time, Anna was finally allowed to pick out her own furniture, which was a big deal for her, she told me years later. She thought that my bedroom had such a pretty bedspread, as well as other feminine touches, whereas her furniture was very plain and looked like it was more for a boy's room. She hated her really ugly, green-plaid bedspread. How she would have loved a different one— more like the one her "little sister" had. But she knew it was best not to ask for a new one. That would be a mistake. She had to be grateful for what she had. She had to learn to keep quiet.

But now, she picked exactly what she wanted—a beautiful Broyhill modern walnut chest and dresser, with a matching bedframe. And she chose a very feminine ruffled, quilted top bedspread, with roses, lilacs, and hydrangeas. My father had talked my mother into letting Anna decorate her own room, but it was more about his contentedness than hers. If a fluffy, feminine bedspread made her more comfortable, that was better for him.

Anna started high school in New Jersey and slowly made friends, a few who would remain her friends for many years. No one, however, knew what was going on with her and my father. He told her it would just be "easier" if she didn't speak of it. So she didn't.

When she turned sixteen, my father implemented new rules for her to follow.

"We have something very special. Something you will never find with another man. Or boy in high school," he told her one night in her bedroom.

"What do you want me to say?" Anna asked.

"You will make sure that when you go on dates in high school, you do not ever let one of those boys touch you. It's acceptable for you to do a quick good-night kiss, but no touching. That is only for me." Anna complied. She found this unsettling, but she didn't know any better. Everything she learned about life, love, and sex was from Arthur.

Chapter 9

Mia

Growing up with my father was not easy. He had little time for me, but I initially thought that was normal for fathers and daughters. I truly would get lost watching *Donna Reed* and *Father Knows Best* and became convinced that as an adult I wanted "to be Donna Reed." But over time I began to see, primarily on television, that fathers really did make time for their daughters. I so badly wanted my father to. But more than that, I wanted him to want to spend time with me.

When I was nine, I had surgery to remove two large, dark, ugly birthmarks on my left leg. It was 1963 and physicians were troubled that they might be a cancer risk. I remember my mother being with me in the hospital but not my father. (She would tell me years later that it was snowing, and he didn't want to clear the driveway and trek in the snow to visit me.) My parents didn't explain to me that after surgery my leg would need to heal, and I would have stitches and bruises and likely pain. When I woke in the recovery room, I expected my left leg to be the mirror image of my right leg. But it wasn't. There were two giant scars with big black stitches and red, purple, yellow, and blue discoloration up and down my leg. And, clearly, the surgeon didn't see how traumatic that was for a nine-year-old as he came into my room with the hideous looking birthmarks in a jar and proudly showed them to me. I threw up. It was inconceivable that a competent surgeon would have no common sense. And that my parents would not have prepared me for post-surgery. At least I didn't have cancer.

Upon returning home from the three-day event, I was completely and utterly upstaged by my mother, who was dragging her ass around the house half-crying and moaning over her diagnosis of mononucleosis. I had no idea what that was, and frankly was too afraid to ask, but I assumed it must have been something pretty terrible for my mother to carry on so much and ignore me just days after a traumatic surgery. I was so worried about my mother and so embarrassed by my ugly leg and was very uncomfortable because of the pain, but I rarely complained. I somehow knew it wouldn't help matters.

A few weeks after the surgery, I was getting very excited about my upcoming tenth birthday party. One afternoon during kickball at school, I was talking with the physical education teacher. Since I wasn't allowed to play kickball yet, I was named "assistant coach," and we were watching the other girls play. A few moments later, one of my girlfriends came running out of the school building as fast as she could, shouting, "President Kennedy just got shot, and he might die." The teacher gathered our team together and initially there was just disbelief. Was this a stupid prank? We all walked back to our respective classrooms and the principal came on the loudspeaker. The president had been shot and died in Dallas earlier that day.

I obviously knew that it was a big tragedy for the president to be assassinated, but I didn't really understand why my mother, who came home from work early, was hysterically crying. The president was dead and that was terrible, but did it mean something personally to my family? Then came the "family shame" that Lee Harvey Oswald was killed by a Jew, Jack Ruby. My mother was inconsolable at this point, and I was very worried that now it might be "a bad thing" to be Jewish. There was no more talk of a birthday party.

Yet there were some happier times in the big house for me and that was when we were playing outside. In the winter, there was so much snow and ice that my neighborhood friends and I would ice-skate and sleigh ride on the little street's front lawns and driveways.

And in the summer, the cul-de-sac would be a wonderful place to play kickball. And we did. For hours. I have no recollection of my parents participating or just watching as I played, when I desperately wanted to show off to them. To show off how well I ice-skated. Or played kickball. To make them proud. Or just to pay attention to me.

Mia McDaniel

Chapter 10

Anna & Rose

At the beginning of every school year, my mother and I went clothes shopping, sometimes with my brother too. Or my mother would make the trip herself and bring back wonderful new blouses, pants, dresses, shoes, and hair ribbons for school. Anna was not taken for new clothes and came to understand that Simon and I were the "real" children. She was an impostor. Yet she had thought it was implicit that once she joined the family, she would be treated as part of the family. Apparently, that was not the case. Once when I gingerly asked her why she didn't get new clothes for school, Anna kindly replied it was because they didn't have her size. I chose to believe her. A pretty grown-up comment for a hurting teenager to make. Even for her senior prom, Anna donned a dress she'd had for two years. She tried so hard not to feel bad about it. My father had even told her that as long as they were together, he would take care of her. Clearly, that did not include new clothes. Nor did it include anything else that this young girl needed to grow up. Taking care of her was not his plan, and it never would be. It was all about him and how he could benefit from her company. My brother and I also suffered because of his selfishness and lack of regard for his children. He was an excellent provider when he and our mother were married. But nothing more.

One afternoon there was a wonderful family gathering. Both Oma and Opa and Nanny and Papa (Arthur's mother and father) visited for a delicious, enormous brunch that my mother exquisitely prepared. I was overjoyed to be surrounded by my family.

And my grandparents and aunt and uncle were paying so much attention to me. Family gatherings hardly ever happened, and I so loved them. The family, the food, everybody dressed up. It was so much fun. I didn't want it to end.

After about an hour of chatting, munching hors d'oeuvres, and drinking, anticipating the many dishes of fabulous food that would soon be served, Nanny asked my mother if they could speak privately. "Of course," her daughter-in-law replied. They went inside, Rose poured some iced tea, and they sat in the comfortable family room with its overstuffed chairs and ornate satin pillows.

"Rose, this is very hard for me to say, but as Arthur's mother, I have to say it. You need to watch your husband because I think there is something going on between him and Anna. It's not kosher. She needs to be out of this house. He is doing things with her that he shouldn't be doing," Nanny told her.

"Are you crazy?" my mother shouted. "I think *you* need to be out of my house." That was the end of the conversation forever.

Years later, when Anna and I got together, Anna said, "Your mother knew damn well what was going on when I was thirteen and fourteen and even older in the next room. How could she not have known? Of course, she knew. If she would have tried to stop it, it would have been the best thing to happen to me. But she didn't. I don't know why. Maybe the shame of it all? It was the sixties and pedophilia was never a topic of discussion. She didn't protect me from his predatory behavior and didn't give much thought to you and your brother either."

Nanny didn't leave the house that afternoon until it was *time* to leave the house. Years later, I learned from my aunt Carol (my father's sister), that this story was true.

Apparently, my nanny begged my father to leave Anna alone. And when she did, he literally screamed at his diminutive, uneducated mother, "It is none of your business. If you don't stop, I will never speak to you again." She knew how angry he was, and he was a bully. He meant what he said. She didn't want to lose him forever. She never brought it up again.

~

I have few memories of gatherings like this one where grandparents, aunts and uncles, and other relatives congregated. I cherished those times we got together. It seemed to me that visiting my oma and opa in Riverdale was pretty much the only time we ever spent with our extended family. I only recall one time when we drove to Scarsdale, where my aunt Carol and uncle Bob lived. My other grandparents were there too, and I was so excited. I was wearing a black and white dress that was my mother's, that I thought was really beautiful and I remember feeling so pretty wearing it. She shortened it and took it in a little so that it fit. That gathering was more than fifty years ago, yet when I randomly think of it, I'm close to tears and feel light-headed. I distinctly remember feeling like an outsider trying so hard to be an insider. I learned many years later that my uncle Bob despised my father because of his immoral behavior and especially the ramifications for me and Simon. It would have been incredibly beneficial for someone to have shared that with me as a young adult. It could have been an enormous boost to my self-esteem. It really wasn't me. It was my father.

~

Anna graduated from high school in 1964. In the fall, she attended Hofstra University, primarily on scholarships. The college was in Hempstead on suburban Long Island. The timing was good. My mother didn't have to think about the conversation with her mother-in-law the year before. Anna was now "out of our house."

My mother repeatedly told me, "Your father and I didn't pay one penny for Anna's education. Not tuition. Not room and board.

Not books." They told me that Anna's mother and stepfather paid for her college. I never understood why they made such a fuss about that. I never thought about that, and I didn't care who paid for Anna's schooling. And wasn't she "one of the kids" anyway? My parents were constantly giving me way too much information.

When Anna started college, our family was once again preparing to move into a bigger, grander, more elegant home that was being custom built for us in Dix Hills, New York, an affluent suburb in the hamlet of Huntington on Long Island. It would take eight to ten months to build and would be our fourth house, the fifth residence for me since I was born. I wasn't even eleven yet. In the meantime, we relocated to a charming, cozy, small, garden apartment (today's townhome) in Huntington. The move from a 3,400-square-foot house to a temporary dwelling of 1,000 square feet was quite an adjustment. But we all thought it was going to be worth it. A fabulous new home would be ready by the following year.

Chapter 11

Mia

Dix Hills would never happen.

My parents argued all day and night. At least that's what it seemed like to me, at eleven and a half. The fights were extremely intense and loud and scary, horrifying. Things were thrown. Voices were raised. One time, my mother went blind for a few days, a psychosomatic blindness, but blind nevertheless. It was awful, never quiet. Maybe at 3:00 a.m. I didn't know what to do, and my "big sister" Anna was in college, and hardly ever visited. It was a very tough time, not only for my parents, but also for me, Simon, and Anna. Anna was terrified that once we left New Jersey for Dix Hills, there would never be a place for her, physically or emotionally again.

Living in that environment of constant hollering and nasty remarks my parents flung at each other was extremely difficult. I didn't want to talk with either one of my parents as I was afraid they would holler at me too. And be nasty to me. I was uncomfortable living in my own house. And it wasn't even my house, but a small apartment until our house was built. I didn't feel especially safe. My safety became of paramount importance to me later in life, likely a result of all the arguments between my parents. I felt like I wasn't important to them—that they didn't hear me—and sometimes didn't see me.

Later on, as an adult, I lived in southern California during the 1994 Northridge earthquake. I was particularly worried about earthquakes because of the lack of control, more than the fear of objects falling on me or crushing me. I felt like there was nobody to protect me, even when my husband was right there and doing his best to ensure that the kids and I stayed safe. It was similar to when I was a child, a teen, and a young adult. My parents were right there, but I didn't feel like they were watching over me, keeping me safe. Helping me to make the right decisions. Helping me to feel comfortable and secure. And I'm pretty sure my brother shared my sentiments, as he was a particularly stressed little boy and an anxious young man.

When we first moved into the garden apartment, I made friends with Holly, a little girl who lived in the apartment complex and was one of my classmates. Her mother was the music teacher. While playing at Holly's one afternoon, I realized I had never met her dad, and I wondered why, so I asked her, "How come I still haven't met your father?" Holly replied, "My parents are divorced. He doesn't live with us." I heard that and didn't want to be friends with her anymore. I didn't want anything to do with her.

It was a time when divorce was a dirty word and a "broken home" was a terrifying concept to me. I wanted to have a family life like *Leave It to Beaver*, *The Danny Thomas Show*, or, my favorite, *The Donna Reed Show*. I couldn't imagine Beaver's father or Danny Thomas leaving their families. I hadn't met a single child who came from divorced parents, and I found it horrifying, demeaning, embarrassing. Not someone you would want to befriend. My parents would be divorced ten months later.

Anna came "home" for a visit one weekend to the Huntington apartment. While driving back from school, a few blocks from the complex, the car directly in front of her hit a black Labrador puppy. By coincidence, unbeknownst to either woman, my mother was three cars behind Anna and shockingly, the puppy was our dog. While my mother saw that it wasn't Anna, when she arrived home, she told us that Anna had hit and killed our puppy. Anna had stopped to tend to our dog, and when she came home later and heard the horrible, false allegation, she begged us to believe her. She loved the dog, and it was a terrible accident that she had nothing to do with. It was a very ugly incident, among many.

Life continued down this awful path of hollering, accusations, and lies. It was only a matter of months before my parents would separate, culminating in their divorce less than a year later. Not only would we not move to the fabulous house under construction, but far worse than that, Simon and I would never live with our mother and father in the same home again. And making matters worse, my parents never discussed with Simon and me that they were separating. We knew our parents argued, loudly sometimes and it often seemed to come out of nowhere. We remembered when we were kids that some days started out so good and calm. We used to drive around northern New Jersey just to look at all the beautiful mansions. My mother and father in the front seat of our fancy, white Ford convertible and Simon and I in the back. More than once our parents were arguing and our mother hollered at our father, "Arthur, stop the car! Let me out!" While Simon and I thought this recurring scene probably didn't play out at our friend's houses, we were quite shocked when our parents eventually told us that my father would be moving somewhere else. In spite of all the arguing, we never expected to be told that they were divorcing.

We were devastated and stunned that our parents wouldn't reunite, and we would soon be children from "a broken family." In fact, I remember being with Oma in the city and running into some of my mother's friends who asked after my parents. Oma's reply was, "Oh, thank you for asking. They're just great. I'll tell them we saw you." My own grandmother was ashamed that her daughter was getting divorced and so she lied to my mother's friends. She wasn't about to talk about that back then. It was a very disturbing moment for me.

It was during this tumultuous time that I met Lisa in eighth grade. Lisa was rich. Her family lived in Huntington on the lake in a big, gorgeous home with a pool table and a big, beautiful dog. But because I was so horrified by Holly's divorced parents, I naturally assumed that as soon as I confessed that my parents were divorced my new friendship with Lisa would be history. It wasn't and it became a running joke our whole lives.

"Lisa, happy thirtieth birthday. Just wanted to call and say hey and I still love you and I'm so grateful that you wanted to be my best friend, even after I told you my parents divorced." Lisa would, of course, respond with, "Oh no. Your parents are divorced? Let me think about this. OK, I guess I'll still be your BFF. Love you too, Mia." We're still besties today, in our sixties, and have been since we were twelve years old.

Mia McDaniel

Chapter 12

Mia & Simon & Rose & Arthur

Immature and very sheltered, Simon and I were plunged into a whole new world. We now had our home with our mother, and our father had his own home. Just like Holly. There wasn't any discussion about "joint custody" either. Instead, it was understood that Simon and I would live with our mother and stay with our father every other weekend and perhaps one weeknight (we found out as adults that our father had not fought for joint custody at all). There was also no, "You better sit down, kids" conversation as in Sonny and Cher's 1967 song that became a mantra for divorced parents. Talk to your kids. Tell them they're loved. They'll always be loved. This isn't because of them. Instead, not a word was spoken. Just, "We're moving. And we'll be living in different places. Your father will be living somewhere else." I would daydream about bringing them back together, like in the 1961 movie *The Parent Trap*.

My father moved into a beautiful one-bedroom apartment in a very stylish high-rise in Forest Hills, Queens. For years, my brother and I remembered his apartment on the seventeenth floor and its spectacular view of five New York City bridges and Shea Stadium, as the Mets' baseball stadium was known.

My mother, Simon, and I moved to Lefrak City in Queens, a complex of twenty seventeen-story buildings (4,605 apartments) for working- and middle-class families who couldn't afford to live in Manhattan or didn't want to live in Manhattan. It was also a haven for divorcees and their children. Plenty of single women for my mother to "run around with" and plenty of single men for her to date. And she had plenty of dates. She was young, beautiful, and eager to remarry.

Unfortunately, she had little discretion and few misgivings about having her beaus spend the night. Or dating married men. It was a very strange and unsettling time for Simon and me. I wondered why you would ever go out with someone who already had a wife. There was one man, the president of a bank in the city, who I felt sure would leave his wife and marry my mother. At least that's what my mother thought and relayed to me, and she was so sad when it didn't happen. Once again, too much information.

I so badly wanted her to find a husband. She told Simon and me about how important it was, and I did everything I could to help her, including embarrassing myself horribly one evening with her then beau. She was very excited that he was coming over because he had been out of the country, and they hadn't seen each other in weeks. She made it clear to us that we had to be on our best behavior around him. I was nervous. The doorbell rang as I was dressing. I thought it was best to answer the door as soon as I possibly could. I ran to the door partially dressed, with my pants on, holding my brown sweater with the beautiful fake pearls on it in front of my body and nearly shrieked, "Hi, Eli. We're so happy to see you," certain that this was the best way to greet him, letting him know I couldn't get dressed fast enough. He was a handsome man, with a big smile, but when he saw me, he looked at me with utter disdain. He looked at me like I was a seductress, just waiting for his entrance. I was only thirteen, a child, and wanted to welcome him for my mother. When I left the room, I was more concerned that I had harmed my mother's relationship with him than I was about the terrible humiliation I felt at the way he glared at me.

My mother met two women in Lefrak City, who would be her friends for years. The three of them were close in age and each of them was divorced with two children. And one of the women's

Mia McDaniel

daughters was a beauty, at eleven. They got together often at each other's apartment or at a man's apartment, whom they had befriended who lived a few floors above us. I often wondered if he would ever be my mother's husband or maybe one of her friends' husbands. I questioned what went on up there, but my mother never wanted to talk about it, so I let it go.

My mother was especially close to one of these women in particular and by all appearances had a fantastic friendship. My mother, however, ruminated on this woman's life constantly. Both to her, and unfortunately, to me. "She dates too much. She doesn't date enough. She needs to ask her ex for more money. She is spending too much money. Like on the color television she bought." She was the first one we knew to have a color TV. While most of the programs were still in black and white, the commercials were primarily in color. Simon and I would spend afternoons with her daughters mostly to watch the ads.

The nearly two years spent in Lefrak City was especially traumatic for me, as I was caught between my parents' inability to be kind and their desire to tout themselves as the far superior parent. For me, it was constant. For Simon, it was less so, only because he was male and too young to bully. My mother never tired of telling me what "a terrible father" and "awful husband" my dad was. Similarly, my father went on ad nauseam about my mother's abhorrent behavior as "a bad mother" and "not a good wife either."

Early on in our very small, two-bedroom, one bath, fourteenth-floor apartment with a very scary terrace protected only by a few steel posts and an ugly metal enclosure, my mother met Raymond (Ray) Casino in the bar/restaurant on the ground floor of our apartment building. It looked like a very nice space that I always thought was very expensive. I didn't know for sure though. My mother never took me or my little brother there for dinner. Or lunch. Or really anywhere for dinner or lunch.

Ray was not Jewish. He was Catholic. But Oma, whose family was murdered in concentration camps, repeatedly told me,

"What matters is to be happy and safe. It doesn't matter to me if you fall in love with a Catholic, a Buddhist, or a Jew. I don't care if he is Black or white or purple." I always thought this was a wonderful, loving sentiment from my beloved grandmother, a Jewish woman who had endured so much.

Unfortunately, Arthur pretended he did not share this perspective (his third wife was not Jewish). Upon hearing that my mother might remarry, he called me and screamed at me for more than twenty minutes claiming, "Mia, your mother and Ray will be damned to hell if they marry. Him being Catholic and her Jewish." Unable to process this new information, I was very troubled by the idea for a long time. I didn't know what it really meant.

But I felt an allegiance toward my mother that can only be explained by the fact that we lived with her and it seemed mandatory. Halfway through the lengthy, unpleasant call, I grabbed my tape recorder and recorded my father to play back to my mother and Ray. I suppose I was looking for some sort of "Brownie points" that never materialized. My mother and father continuously played with my emotions, trying to make me despise the other parent. It was an extremely difficult way to live.

In their never-ending attempts to "outdo" each other with nasty insults aimed at their former spouse, there were a number of very uncomfortable situations they placed me in. A most appalling incident, instigated by my mother, was at my aunt Carol's wedding shower. I was invited to join my father at the big celebration at a very fancy country club that for years remained the most beautiful place I'd ever seen. I was so young and impressionable and really hadn't been anywhere comparable. I was excited that my nanny and papa and my uncle Jerry and aunt Jean (Arthur's brother and sister-in-law) and other relatives, as well as my aunt's grown-up friends, would be there. It was going to be so much fun, and my mother bought me a new dress for the occasion too. (My mother always made sure Simon and I were dressed well when we saw our father, even when she could barely afford it.) She thought it was particularly important at this large gathering of his family.

Before my dad picked me up, my mother sat me down and said, "There is something I would like you to say at your aunt's party. If you love me, Mia, you will say it."

Being fully aware of the guest list, my mother said, "I want you to tell your father while everyone is eating that I went to the drugstore for medication when you and Simon had tonsillitis, and the pharmacist told me that your father didn't pay the bill and until he did, I couldn't get your medicine."

I was not a bit comfortable with this and felt pretty certain that it would embarrass my father. But I knew I had no choice. I had to say it. I told my mother that I would. She told me that if I loved her, I would indict him. I did love my mother. But I loved my father too.

I nervously waited for the quiet time while everyone was eating and blurted it out loud enough for the table of twenty-four to hear.

It was one of very few times in my young life that I remember my father being calm and kind and gentle with me. "I'll take care of it, Mia. Don't worry." And that was that. Until the next time.

There was one evening when I just didn't wash the dishes, do the ironing, or make sure my brother took his bath, like I was supposed to every night. I think it was some sort of protest. I was going to do it, but my mother came home fifteen minutes early that night.

When she hollered at me and forced my brother in the tub right away, she exploded that I couldn't have possibly done all my chores in fifteen minutes. I had no answer. I was both proud and ashamed. I never did that again.

I was acutely aware that my mother worked very hard. She was a gift buyer at Bergdorf Goodman's in the city. She really liked her job, but soon her dream job materialized. She was hired as a ground hostess for El Al Airlines (Israel's national airline) at Kennedy airport. It was glamorous and exciting, and there would likely be an opportunity to meet eligible single men. She was so excited and called her best friend as soon as she returned home: "Wait 'til you hear this. I just got a new job. I'll be working for El Al Airlines at JFK. I'm thrilled! It'll be the most exciting job I've ever had and I can't wait!"

"Congratulations, Rose. Wow. You might meet some handsome, rich Jewish men. Pilots. Or passengers. They're going to have to have friends for me and all of our other friends. When do you start? What are you days or your specific hours? Do you have a schedule yet?"

"My regular schedule will be early evenings, likely five until early morning around two, but for the first two weeks, it will be nine to five."

"You're going to be leaving Mia and Simon alone at night?"

"Mia is thirteen. She can handle taking care of Simon and herself. What's the big deal?"

"Rose, that's a big adjustment for her. She's already struggling with your divorce and let's face it, she's a terrific kid, but not very mature. I think this is going to be very hard for her."

"She's just going to have to get used to it. I'll make dinners and freeze them. So she'll just have to heat the oven and feed her brother and make sure he takes a bath. The only chore she has now is the ironing. I just won't be in the apartment with them. I don't think it's that big of a deal." She hung up and thought about how she would tailor her uniform that evening to hug all the sexy places because she was proud of her youthful, attractive shape.

Her friend was skeptical. She knew her own daughters would not be happy about this, since her oldest was about my age. It was too much responsibility in too short of a time span. She felt my mother was trying to force me to grow up too fast. I was still adjusting to having my parents live in separate places. She also knew that there was absolutely no talking my mother out of it.

My mother's dream job was my nightmare. But I tried to convince myself that it really wasn't so bad and that because she would freeze our dinners every night and make them look like TV dinners, we were lucky. Still, I was an insecure, frightened, and unhappy child (at thirteen, I was more like a girl of nine), and now I was forced to take care of my eight-year-old brother and "protect" him and me until at least three in the morning. Just the two of us in our little fourteenth-floor apartment in the dark. For the next forty years, I was afraid of the dark.

Her dream job lasted only ten months. The Six-Day War broke out and the airline was forced to lay off many of their newest hires, my mother being one of them. She cried for days. I hid my emotions, but I wanted to shout from the rooftops. Such happiness that my mother wouldn't have to work nights. And relief. Simon was eight and just accepted what went on, as he did so well his whole life. Or at least he pretended to. I didn't tell Simon how traumatic it was for me during our mother's El Al employment because he was too young and wouldn't have understood. It wasn't until we began talking more frequently about our parents' behavior that I eventually brought it up. He was very compassionate toward me and very grateful that I was the oldest child and hid so much from him for so many years.

Throughout our tenure in Lefrak City, my mother had no clue how Simon and I were doing with the divorce and subsequent remarriage. She didn't ask. I wanted to talk to her about the divorce and tried to, but with no luck. "You know, your divorce from my father was very difficult for me and Simon, and we had a very hard time growing up. Everything we thought we knew changed. And for the worse. We didn't understand what was really behind the divorce or if one of us did something wrong. Maybe we partially caused it."

My mother's brief response was, "Mia, it was my divorce, not yours. It wasn't about you and really shouldn't have affected you."

When my parents had issues that clearly involved me, I wasn't allowed to "own" any feelings. If it involved them in any way, it was not my hurt, it was theirs, and I shouldn't expect any sympathy from them. Or compassion. Or help. Even the misery over my parent's divorce was "not mine." Throughout my life, I had a very tough time dealing with loss. Whether it was my beloved Oma, my soulmate Michael, or my precious dog, Sir Mick, I often cried and was tormented far longer than I knew was healthy or "normal."

$\sim$

As married adults, Simon and I watched as divorce became commonplace. In the seventies and eighties, divorces peaked at 50 percent of all marriages. In 2021, it fell to a still-staggering 40 percent. Simon divorced in 2005, and I divorced in 2011. Simon had no kids, and, at the time of my divorce, my children were in their early twenties. Similar to my own father, who had moved to California just eighteen months after he and my mother separated, Sam and Michael's father moved to the opposite coast less than three months after we separated.

Even though they were grown, they were shocked and saddened that their dad moved so far away, so soon. His love affair with New York City never waned, even after almost thirty years in Los Angeles.

In the nineties, Simon and I watched as many of our friends got divorced and had all out "bloody custody battles." Some in court. Why didn't our father do that? Why did he settle for every other weekend and one occasional weeknight? And just two weeks in the summer? Is that what all divorced dads did in the sixties? That's what Simon and I thought, and we always gave him far more of a pass than he was entitled to have.

Before departing for California, it seemed to Simon and me that our father was actually trying to be a better parent than when he was married to our mother. He joined "Parents without Partners." While it was not founded or operated as a dating service, parents mingled outside of the activities, and he was often the center of attention when around attractive, single women. Though he did prefer single women without children.

He took us out to some really fun places through Parents without Partners, on his own, or with a date. We went to West Point, The New

Mia McDaniel

York Car show, Hudson River cruises, movies, the theater (including our first-ever play, Mary Martin in *Peter Pan*), and lunches and dinners in Greenwich Village. He was "a Disneyland Dad" for the short time that he lived only twenty minutes from my mother and Simon and me. And he did meet a lot of single women.

It was fun spending the weekends with Daddy. There were morning pancakes, evening Jiffy Pop with way too much melted butter, and lots of Coca-Cola, and he let us stay up as late as we could keep our eyes open. We tried so hard every time to keep them open for "The Million Dollar Movie," a series that featured top movies and wasn't over until around midnight. Then, if you managed to stay up until the very end, you could watch the "Indian Head test pattern"— the television sign-off every night after the national anthem. With our mother, we were never allowed to stay up that late. Not even on weekends.

But Daddy's apartment was only for fun. For snacks. For sodas. For ice cream sundaes with way too much whipped cream and almost a jar of hot fudge sauce. It was never a place for any substantive discussions or sharing of emotions. The hurt we felt, the lack of understanding of how our young lives would go forward, and the mixed emotions we were trying to sort out were not something you approached with Daddy. Not ever. Our father was a young (thirty-six), handsome, newly single parent. And, for the most part, that was all that mattered to him. And money. Although, he would always be stingy with his child support and alimony, at least according to our mother, who frequently complained about how broke we were and how our father was anything but broke. It was a steady stream of bitching that I was never comfortable hearing. Not because I didn't believe it. I honestly didn't know what to believe. I just didn't want to be privy to it. It was too much information that I had never wanted to know.

Whenever I innocently revealed something personal to my father, he would end up mocking me. Years later when my brother and I were visiting him in California, I was much more excited than you would think a sixteen-year-old would be about lunching alone with her father. But I badly craved his time and attention. Still. While talking about adjusting to our new lives, I mentioned that it was very difficult for my mother. I explained that I understood there was a stigma attached to divorced women. They were labeled "divorcées" and often looked upon as promiscuous and over-sexed, not the kind of woman a man would want to marry. For my divorced father, however, he was considered quite eligible. He was very kind and tried to cheer me up. Two days later, he exploded and told me that he was surprised and upset that I would talk about my mother when we were out to lunch. "Maybe if she had been a better wife, she wouldn't be alone right now," he said, even though she had initiated the divorce.

He was often cruel. Another time, when I was twenty-five, living in Manhattan Beach, I was able to buy a brand-new car. I wanted a VW convertible, and I went to the Manhattan Beach dealership by myself and financed a brand-new red Super Beetle, with a beige convertible top. I was so excited and so very proud. I paid too much and hadn't a clue how to negotiate, but I did it. I couldn't wait to drive to Northridge and show my father and his third wife, Joanne. I pulled up, ran inside, and dragged him outside to see my new car. His response? "That's terrific, Mia. What do you want me to do? Have a celebration? I was thirty-one before I could afford my first car because I had a wife and two kids. How fortunate for you." I was devastated. Why did I always expect a different outcome? Where there's life, there's hope, I guess.

Chapter 13

Anna & Arthur

One morning at our father's apartment, when I was looking in the linen closet for my favorite red and white striped towel, I noticed about a half dozen pairs of women's panties and a few bras. I didn't think much of it. But they did look familiar. "I've seen that underwear before. It's not my mother's. But I know I've seen it," I thought to myself, almost out loud. It didn't make that much of an impact though, and I forgot about it. A few days later, when I was looking for my shoes in the hall closet, I randomly opened the left sliding door instead of the right and noticed a few blouses and dresses hanging there. And two coats. And five pairs of women's shoes. Then, I spotted my very favorite pink and green blouse of Anna's. That's it. I realized all the clothes and shoes and bras and panties were Anna's. I was bewildered. Why on earth were Anna's clothes and shoes in my daddy's closet? I couldn't imagine why. At thirteen, I was very innocent. Nothing untoward occurred to me. I was sure there was a simple explanation. And my father was lightning fast in providing it. Another gigantic lie in his ongoing stream of lies.

"Daddy, why are Anna's panties and bras underneath the towels? And I saw her dresses and blouses in our closet."

Without missing a beat, my father said, "Anna's apartment at school is very, very small so I let her keep some of her stuff here."

I thought that was so sweet and caring and couldn't wait to tell my mother about it when he dropped us home on Sunday night.

"Mommy, Daddy is so nice. He lets Anna keep her clothes at his apartment, even though he has a pretty small place and doesn't have a lot of room. She keeps her stuff in the linen closet and at the end of our closet in the hall."

My mother turned white, and in one of the few moments that she demonstrated kindness while speaking about my father, she replied with a curt, "Yes, Mia. That's very nice of your father."

As an adult, I found it shocking that I believed his giant lie. Why didn't it occur to me that it would have been impossible for Anna to change her blouse or even her panties if they were at my father's house? One of my therapists over the years insisted that I must have known subconsciously that his explanation was untrue. She was wrong. I had no idea at all. And once I did, I wouldn't believe it for more than thirty years.

Mia McDaniel

Chapter 14

Rose & Anna & Mia

I am absolutely certain that after I told my mother about finding Anna's clothing in my father's apartment, she began spreading hideous lies about my cousin to anyone who would listen. She changed the narrative so that now, Anna was no longer her cousin and my grandmother's young and vulnerable niece, whose father committed suicide and who had spent a year in an Israeli orphanage. Nor was she abused by my mother's husband and the father of her children. No. Anna became the "ungrateful, self-centered vixen who calculatedly and knowingly went after her husband and stole him right from under her innocent nose." Any other explanation was too despicable to comprehend. Too terrible to think that her husband of more than eleven years was fucking her first cousin. And she was in the next bedroom when he went into Anna's room. With their two children down the hall. Under their gorgeous roof. In their dreamy sixties suburbia.

It was the beginning of the reality that my mother tried so hard for years to pretend was not really happening. Her ex-husband was now enjoying her cousin Anna's company as an overnight guest. The cousin who lived with us for years as the oldest child. Now, she was regularly spending the night in his apartment. The apartment where Simon and I stayed. Did she stay when we were there? Did that even matter to her? The drama never ended. What the fuck was going on? She had to know. Simon and I had no idea.

How could my father have done that to my mother? How could he have done that to me and Simon? How could he have done that to Anna? How could he continue this deception and shameless conduct? It's no wonder that Simon and I had issues with the opposite sex when our father had no boundaries and our mother spent more time looking for a new husband than caring for her children.

For Anna, it was simple to do what my father asked, though she wasn't always comfortable. But she thought if she did what he wanted, she would always have a place to live, and she thought he loved her and he was her protector. She couldn't imagine he would do anything that wasn't in her best interest. He was a good dad to me and Simon, she thought at the time. He wouldn't hurt her for anything.

Yet, she was an innocent child from another country, only living in America for less than four years. Speaking English for less than four years. Learning to navigate New York and New Jersey for less than four years. And the handsome, strong, loving head of the family wanted her to be somebody else? She didn't have any choice. And he kept saying that it was okay. It was all good. It was all about love. How could there be anything wrong with it? I'm sure Anna felt that she must have been a very special girl, because she believed that my father loved her more than anyone else in the whole wide world.

It was a long, slow painful process for everyone, especially Anna. She was a little girl when her "cousin" (by marriage) started selfishly using her. For whatever he wanted, whenever he wanted it. Telling her how much he loved her and how they were meant to be together. Certainly not as father and daughter. But as girlfriend and boyfriend? Maybe more than that?

The entire time that my father was abusing this child, I was wholly in the dark, completely unaware that anything in our home might be pernicious. I was stunned and horrified to learn the truth.

Then, my sweet little brother Simon became convinced that Anna abused him. After all, doesn't that always happen? The abused abuses? It took him years of therapy to understand that it never happened. On some level as a child, he was aware that sexual deviance was taking place in his home. He misplaced this subconscious awareness of his father's aberrant behavior on to Anna, who was so sad that he thought that was even possible.

Growing up watching *The Donna Reed Show* and *Father Knows Best*, the show's outcome almost always reflected well on the father. He was most often thought of as the hero. Hero to the mother. Hero to the kids. Hero to the next-door neighbor. As an adult, I was convinced that every book, every television drama, every dramatic movie, or engaging play would "come around" to the father trying so hard to be the good guy, even when he clearly wasn't. He could be portrayed as the worst bastard in the world, but before the show was over, there would always be the "AHA moment" when he would apologize to his wife, even if he did commit the murder. Or beg for his daughter's forgiveness. He would confess to the next-door neighbor that he did the dirty deed, but he really wasn't so bad.

I think that's why I gravitated to the darker side when it came to picking movies or television shows. And books and plays. I didn't like musicals. I disdained rom-coms. The shows with evil, despicable plots drew my attention. I love Joyce Carol Oates, and not only because I believe her writing is the best, but because her books tend to be dark, ugly, confusing. Often with themes of parental abuse. I began to understand that not all daughters were cherished by their dads. Not all men were good. Sometimes the father or the boyfriend or the husband really was the villain or the pedophile or the rapist. But he nearly always apologized, confessed, or promised to change. That "AHA moment." My father and I never, ever had one.

A few months before my father's death in 2016, Simon was at my father's apartment, and he finally confronted him about what he had done. "You fucking blew up our family. You slept with Anna when she was just a child and then you married her and further tore us all apart. It wasn't just about you and my mother and Anna. What about me and Mia? Where's my fucking apology and your contrition?" he said.

"Okay, fine. I'm sorry. I shouldn't have done that. Are we done now?"

Chapter 15
Anna & Arthur

When Anna went off to college at eighteen, her indoctrination as my father's paramour was pretty secure. An attractive, intelligent, scholarship student, she was frequently asked on dates. She finally decided to accept one of these dates with an assistant professor. They went out for a few weeks and really enjoyed each other's company. It was the first time she had sex with anyone other than my father. She was twenty-one.

In 2017, she told me, "I felt so guilty about having sex with someone else. But we had such a good relationship, and he was only three years older than me. He treated me well, but I was so anxious and nervous when I wasn't with him. Thinking about what your father would do. I was by myself one Saturday in a mall near school and my mind was racing. I felt faint and I passed out. I woke up in your father's car. Someone must have looked in my wallet to get his phone number—on one of those old-fashioned emergency cards we used to put in wallets—because he was driving me to a physician friend of your aunt Carol's."

They were worried she might have epilepsy because a bystander said, "It looked like she had had a seizure." After numerous tests over a few weeks, it was determined that she had "suffered an event," and she never had another. But the consequences she faced with my father were disturbing when she felt she had no choice but to tell him about her relationship with another man.

"Arthur, I think I fainted because I have been so scared to tell you, and so scared and guilty in my own head because I have been having a relationship with a man in college," she confessed. She couldn't live with the secret anymore. How he had twisted her inside and out. She was nearly hysterical crying and was terrified he would leave her. For good.

My father could barely contain himself. Could barely speak civilly. "How could you do this to me? What the fuck were you thinking? This isn't a game. You are not ever to dare go out with anyone but me. You are mine. Do you understand me?" She responded, but he could scarcely hear her "yes." He then promised he would drive to campus more often and take her to his apartment in Forest Hills more frequently. The trip was only forty minutes. But he didn't promise that he would stop dating other women. He was sure she didn't know. My brother and I didn't see her so we wouldn't be telling her. And there was nobody else to worry about. Or muzzle.

While there was a certain amount of security, familiarity, and comfort, Anna was completely baffled. Does he "own her" now? Was she committed to being with him for the rest of her life? Was this what she wanted? Did she even know what she wanted? He had taught her everything. Everything. Maybe this was the best news she ever heard. Please, God, it had to be.

But dating college guys was interesting and even fun. She loved making new acquaintances and she had similar interests with college boys her age. With Arthur there existed that significant age difference. She was in her early twenties and he was in his late thirties. And there were plenty of other issues, like he was separated from a thirteen-year-marriage, and he had two children.

And to complicate matters further, his children were her cousins. This was irrelevant with respect to Anna, however, because she had idolized Arthur since she was a very young girl and knew nothing else.

For Arthur, there was no problem. At long last, she was as finely tuned as a Stradivarius to meet his, and only his, needs. He'd been "teaching" her for years to become his ideal woman.

Chapter 16
Mia

I was so sad being in the small apartment with my mother and brother and having my dad living somewhere else. I never got to be with "my sister" Anna. She was away at college. And at that time, I didn't know she spent most of her free time with my father. We didn't know when, if ever, we would get to see her again.

This was my new life—no gradual transition—but a child who two years before was preparing to move to a grand, new, custom-built house, with my two parents living together, a live-in maid, and "an older sister" visiting from college.

That said, our small apartment had some benefits. In the daytime, because it was so densely populated and most families were divorced or widowed, I made friends with girls who shared comparable situations, whose fathers lived in separate residences.

Family life, however, was increasingly difficult. Early on when my mother worked days, she expected me to do things that children should not have to do by themselves. Particularly, since I experienced every second of my parents' miserable divorce and was told to adjust almost overnight.

There was one specific appointment that I found especially distressing. My mother told me that the school required all students to go to a doctor for a check-up and they would allow us to take the time off during a school day to do so. I really wanted my mother to be there with me, but I knew that was not going to happen. My mother would not accompany Simon and me to medical appointments if it meant taking time off work. I believed then and still feel today that she absolutely should have made arrangements to take me. She could have gone to work late or left her job early or called in sick or told her boss the truth about her daughter's physical. I really needed her and wanted her by my side and I'm sure she understood that. I was terrified that I would have to get undressed in front of a strange man. Even though I was a little embarrassed, I asked my mother if I would have to do that. She knew how scared I was of being naked. "No, sweetheart. You will not have to get undressed. Don't worry."

Armed with that information, I went to the doctor, far less afraid than I was before talking with my mother. At least now I knew for sure I wouldn't have to take my clothes off. I walked to the physician a few blocks away and when he came into the examining room, he told me to do just that. There was no nurse present. I started to cry and told him my mother said I wouldn't have to undress. "Well, you do," he replied and began to take my clothes off himself. Without consent. And without someone else present.

It was horrible. I was a sobbing, frightened twelve-year-old girl, too afraid to fight him or run out. He was a doctor, and I knew I would embarrass my mother and make her angry if I did that. I sat there and wept while he examined me and went home traumatized. When my mother came home from work, I was crying and told her through tears about the awful, disturbing incident of having a man undress me himself. I expected her to go there the next day. Maybe with the police. Instead, my mother laughed and said, "What's the big deal? He's a doctor, Mia. He sees everyone naked. Your body is no different." I felt utterly betrayed and, to this day, have trouble disrobing for medical examinations by male physicians.

Another troubling visit was to the dentist. I was in the eighth grade and couldn't recall ever visiting a dentist. I walked the few blocks to the dentist. I was escorted to the exam room and sat in the big chair. At least I wouldn't have to take off my clothes. The dentist had some instruments on the little shelf that swung in front of me and he looked in my mouth. After a few minutes he nearly shouted, "You have twenty-six cavities, young lady." Having no concept of how many cavities were normal to have, I assumed I far exceeded that amount. Years later I asked my mother why she didn't take me to the dentist sooner. Or go with me on that doctor's appointment. She exclaimed, "I had to work."

In the eighties, I worked for myself, full-time from my home office (initially, the breakfast nook) so I could raise our children (my husband worked very long hours and frequently had to go out of town), and I occasionally thought about my mother's answer regarding the terrible dental appointment. I just could not understand how my mother could have neglected to take me and Simon to the dentist.

And I paid for that my entire life with so many dental issues. I know that there are many parents who simply cannot take off work for a child's medical appointment because they don't have the funds, or they don't have jobs. Some families have no insurance and no "village" to help. But that wasn't the case for us. Rather, my mother should have made arrangements to take me. It was simply selfish, bad parenting. As it was with the physician. When I had children, I was so over the top in my protecting them and, because of my experience with the physician, I was worried that my daughter would be uncomfortable with a male doctor and that perhaps my son would never allow a female physician to examine him. I didn't want them to be just like me. But they weren't because their father and I made sure they had a safe environment when they were growing up.

Mia McDaniel

Chapter 17

Rose

There were several times when my mother's behavior concerned me, but I didn't quite understand it. She was very pretty and often used her good looks as a weapon around men. When she and her girlfriends were worried that Sam Lefrak, the owner of Lefrak City, was going to raise the rents, she decided to pay him a visit. She was absolutely stunning and gorgeous in a black-and-white striped business suit, with a very short skirt and a huge artificial red rose on her lapel. I had never seen my mother dressed like that before, and I thought she looked like she had walked straight out of a fashion magazine. A very sexy fashion magazine. I was also a little uncomfortable that my mother was dressed like that, and it looked to me like a little too much of her boobs were on display. At this time, my mother was thirty-one years old. Who knew how old Lefrak City's owner was?

She came home hours later. We would be moving soon. The meeting with the real estate tycoon was never discussed again. Clearly, it hadn't gone the way she hoped.

A few years later I was looking for a sweater in my mother's closet and saw her beautiful suit on a hanger in the back. I thought about how gorgeous and sexy she looked that day. Maybe even sexier than at any other time, including dressing up to go out with her boyfriends. I felt embarrassed that she dressed like that for a meeting with an important and powerful man. I wished she would have dressed more appropriately.

It reminded me of when we lived in the big house in New Jersey and my fourth grade teacher (who all the girls thought was so handsome) wanted us to learn to play the flutophone (a wind instrument made of lightweight plastic that requires little breath force, unlike an actual flute or clarinet) in one night. I was very worried because I couldn't figure out how to do it and was scared to go to school the next day. My mother told me not to worry because she would meet with the teacher first thing in the morning and work it all out. She did. But I remember being surprised that she was very dressed up and looked quite beautiful. Just for a meeting with my teacher. And she wouldn't provide any details. She just told me to go to class and it would all be fine.

Chapter 18
Rose & Ray

After being married to Ray for a few months, with our tight quarters getting even tighter, it was time to move again, for the seventh time. This time to Edgewater, New Jersey, a lovely little community on the Hudson River, with a view of New York City—if you got one of the good houses. My mother, brother, and Ray moved into the large townhouse, while I spent a few weeks living with one of my friend's and her family in Lefrak City to finish eighth grade.

About this time I told my mother again that Simon and I were sad and scared after the divorce and I wanted to talk about it. I wanted some reassurance that we hadn't caused it. Her brief response hadn't changed, "Mia, it was my divorce, not yours. It wasn't about you and really shouldn't have affected you." Decades later when I was about forty-five, my mother told me that she had been watching *Oprah* and the subject was grown children of divorce, and she said she should have realized that it had consequences for her children. I guess it took her more than thirty years to understand that basic concept. I appreciated her candor, but knew it was self-serving. Oprah made her feel guilty.

The new home was dark and dreary. The front door was below the street level. No view of New York City for us. It was a pretty large apartment with three bedrooms and it had a huge rooftop where I could often be found, when I came back home from staying at my girlfriend's house. I loved spending hours there, sunbathing with a deep, dark tanning lotion, a Fresca, and some Fritos, while reading Truman Capote's *In Cold Blood*. The book was on the assigned summer reading list, but I have often wondered about how appropriate it was for such young students to read the gruesome book. In researching the issue, I found that it all came down to the students' maturity, and I, for one, was far too immature to be reading Truman Capote's masterpiece. I remember hiding the book from my parents as I was afraid they would scold me for reading it, even though it had been assigned.

Perhaps this frightening book became another early example of my preference for the darker side of books and every other form of entertainment.

While living in Edgewater, my little brother was brutally bitten by a neighbor's German shepherd. It was a terrible accident, and he was taken by ambulance to the hospital with my mother. I wasn't back home yet, but my brother wanted me to be with him more than anything else, so my friend's father took me home that evening.

Simon and I became even closer. We realized that we really needed each other. We suffered great trauma because of our self-absorbed, neglectful parents, coupled with a new stepfather within a year and a half of our parents' divorce. And soon, our dad would relocate to California. Another big disappointment. Why were our parents so unconcerned about us? Why did they have children? Would I be able to be a good mother?

Ray was more blue collar than white collar. He was an excellent salesman and rather quickly landed a job selling furniture at JC Penney, while my mother worked retail in the jewelry section of a department store nearby. They were struggling financially. And emotionally. Apparently, Ray had neglected to pay his ex-wife child support for their two children, and he owed her for almost a year and a half. He didn't have the money, though I wondered if he would have paid it if he had it. We didn't even know he had children.

Early one evening, there was a loud knock on the front door. Before answering the door, my mother looked in the peephole and

Mia McDaniel

saw two local cops. "It's the Edgewater Police. We're looking for Raymond Casino. We have a search warrant," an enormous man in blue announced. Ray had broken the law. Multiple times. It had been far too long since he had paid child support. Far longer than the suspected eighteen months.

My mom quickly told Simon and me that Ray would be hiding in the attic. "Please. It's very important that you do not talk to the police. If they ask you where Ray is, you do not know. Work, maybe? Please. This is very important," she pleaded.

An officer asked me where Raymond was, and I repeated what my mother told me to say. They didn't ask little Simon. The cops searched the apartment but didn't find Ray. They didn't check the attic. They left, leaving my mom with some paperwork for him. That was the last time I heard anything about Ray's children or his ex-wife. Or pretty much anything else about his life before 1965.

Chapter 19

Mia & Simon & Rose & Ray

Simon and I remembered driving to Miami Beach from our New Jersey house in the summer for two straight years when we were little, and we stayed in a beachfront hotel for a week. It was the only time our parents, as a married couple, took us almost anywhere. Now my mother was telling us that we were moving to Miami Beach. I wondered if we would be living in some posh hotel. Or, were we evading the Edgewater police? Maybe it was simply a terrible financial situation for my family. All I really knew was that it was 1968 and this was the eighth time I moved in my life and I wasn't even fifteen yet.

No, we weren't going to live in some posh hotel. Or a wonderful new house. Thank God for our Oma and Opa.

My grandparents were coming to their beloved daughter's rescue again. They bought a lovely four-family house in south Miami Beach with the Bay at the end of the cul-de-sac. They occupied one of the first-floor apartments and my mother, Ray, Simon, and I were going to live in one of the units upstairs.

Our apartment needed to be painted and a few minor repairs needed to be made before we could move in. It wasn't expected to take too long, a few weeks at most.

My mother and stepfather rented an apartment about two miles away. It only had one-bedroom, but it was just for three weeks, and we couldn't afford anything bigger. It was very small. And very, very hot. Every night, I cried softly in the roll-away bed set up for me in the living room next to Simon. It was awful. I was so miserable and so sad. The apartment was furnished with ugly, dreary, old furniture and the place smelled stale. I felt like I could cry all the time but knew better. I instinctively knew I couldn't talk about it with my mother or Ray. Or my father (who would likely privately gloat). At bedtime, I would look out the window and see the Miami Beach City Hall. I went out of my way years later just to avoid seeing that building, bringing back the dreadful memories. And I couldn't help but wonder why we moved right away. Why couldn't we wait until our apartment was ready? Were the police in New Jersey after our new stepfather? Is that why we left in such a hurry?

In a few weeks, I was going to start another high school in another city, making (I hoped) another group of friends. It was exhausting. Again. And 1968's South Miami Beach was not today's South Miami Beach. It was old, depressing, and very sad, and I was afraid I would hate Miami Beach High School.

Before moving to Florida, my mother told me, "All the girls in Miami Beach have short hair. It's so hot and short hair is so fashionable today."

"But I don't want to cut my hair. I think it looks good. And it's the longest it's ever been. I love it." I said.

My mother didn't care that at fifteen I should be allowed to make my own decision regarding the length of my hair. She told me that I was going to cut my long, brown locks. She insisted. I had no choice. I got the haircut and hoped that it would help me fit in even better, as my mother had told me, and make it easier to make friends. I'd never had such short hair before and I hated it. There wasn't even enough hair to make a ponytail.

When school started in September, I was shocked to see that my mother had lied to me. Nearly all of my very wealthy, beautiful classmates had long, gorgeous, blonde, brown, brunette, and red hair. Not a good start for someone like me, who was already extremely insecure and feeling inferior. Not unlike Anna had felt at my age.

There were only two bedrooms in our new apartment, so Opa built a partition in the larger of the two so that Simon and I could have our own space. It didn't go all the way to the ceiling and you had to walk through my half to get to Simon's. Nevertheless, it afforded all the privacy we needed for dressing, but little else. You could hear every word spoken by either of us.

The Miami Beach apartment looked the same as every other home my brother and I had ever lived in. My mother schlepped the same old furniture and tchotchkes to every house. There was the little corner wooden table that was painted silver gray. Then a white. Then sea foam green. The end table that was round and painted dark blue. Then black. There was the ubiquitous pink, oval Swedish cutting board that hung on the kitchen wall. And the faux brick contact paper as a backsplash in every single kitchen. In every single apartment. Sometimes I truly admired my mother for redoing all the old stuff, trying to make it new. After all, she was always on a tight budget. Except now, she didn't have to pay rent. I wanted it to look different. Newer. Fresher. But mostly different, like she cared about making it a little more special for her kids. A brand-new look for a brand-new place, where we didn't want to be might have helped.

My mother did put wallpaper up on my side of the partition, which I liked. It looked like black and white clouds. It was pretty. And for my sixteenth birthday, she bought me a pink princess telephone. I didn't have my own phone line at the time, but at least I did have my own phone. Most of my friends at Beach High had their own lines, but those families also owned some of the biggest hotels on Collins Avenue. And car dealerships. And shops. I would learn many years later that my experience at Beach High was not unlike the kids at Beverly Hills High who lived on the outskirts or were bussed into Beverly Hills. For me, it wasn't so much about not having the money that most of my friends had. It was about feeling insecure and sad and alone so often. Even though I made friends at Beach High, I rarely ever felt that I was good enough.

Soon after my high school graduation, my mother was extremely kind and caring to me. A boy I was dating for a short while, whom I really liked, said he met someone else. He crushed me and I thought I would never recover. A universal feeling among most teenage girls when relationships don't go as they'd hoped. My mother tried to explain to me that at seventeen, "I had the world by the tail," an expression I eventually grew to despise because it became my mother's "go-to" phrase whenever I had an issue. Any issue. But for that breakup, she was kind and caring. She assured me, saying, "This is not going to be catastrophic. You'll date so many more boys before you meet the man you'll marry. I promise you. Come sit next to me. It's going to be okay. He didn't deserve you anyway."

That talk was one of the few times that she actually sat down and spoke from her heart with me about life and love. She didn't normally make time to bond with me. She wasn't mean. She just wasn't available because everything was always about her. And then it became an easier way out to just say, "You've got the world by the tail." No matter what the problem.

When Ray first started working in Miami, he struggled to create a scenario that would help him overcome his lack of confidence and afford him more opportunities to be successful and make lots of money for his brand-new family. He desperately wanted to impress my mother and my grandparents. He thought it was an excellent idea to say he was a widower. He would explain that the woman with two children whom he had recently married had just died. A struggling widower with two children, suddenly relocated 1,000 miles from home was bound to incur sympathy and maybe help close more sales. That was his loathsome idea. After working there for two months, he told his colleagues that his dear, sweet, beautiful wife had died, and he was working extra hard to support her two children. He also told customers. Colleagues felt so bad for him that some of them told customers or tried to steer customers in his direction. It was working. No, he didn't murder his wife; he just lied about her death. The awakening occurred when my mother picked up the mail and saw a stack of cards for Ray. She opened one. Then another. And another. They were sympathy cards. "You have mail, you asshole! What the hell is this? Sympathy cards for me? What did you fucking do?"

"Rose, I needed a little help in my new gig. I figured I could get some sympathy if I played a sad, lonely widower, whose wife died after a few months of marriage. Is that so bad?"

"Of course that's bad. You're a moron. Who does that? Don't talk to me until you clear this up."

"I'll figure it out, I really don't think it's that awful. In fact, I think this got me some sales."

His colleagues were expressing their sincere sympathies on the death of his lovely wife who was alive and pissed off. I never found out if the truly hideous scheme was uncovered to be the despicable hoax it was, or if Ray just continued the lie. I didn't want to know and knew if I asked my mother, who had revealed the lie in the first place, she would tell me. She told me and Simon everything. Everything we didn't want to know. At the same time, my mother was working at a bank in the posh neighborhood of Surfside. She was a new accounts manager and was trying to get promoted to public relations and marketing. The job in Surfside was her second position at a bank and she knew she had more to offer. In two short years, she earned her promotion as the bank's new public relations and marketing assistant with real potential to grow. She was thriving. Ray was floundering. And us kids? Who knew?

In 1970, my mother and stepfather developed a new strategy they thought would evolve into a highly profitable business. Nightclub tours on South Miami Beach. At that time, there were only two other firms operating such tours, or "crawls." The larger operator was rumored to be run by the Mafia. Naïve as Ray and Rose were, they presumed that it was either just a rumor, or it was an obstacle they could overcome.

Miami Beach was the place to see or be seen in the late 1950s and through the mid-1960s. In the late sixties, however, its popularity declined in a big way. Miami Beach became the mecca for old, sick retirees. Even the once glamorous Lincoln Road that was three blocks from our apartment was no longer chic or glamorous. It was just a half-dozen or so blocks with old, battered shops and restaurants that fewer and fewer customers frequented. This scenario didn't especially help the fledgling business, but its lightning-fast failure was more political and about Mafia control than the deteriorating Miami Beach.

Ray got a job driving a bus in Miami Beach so he could familiarize himself with the city and eventually network so they could hire buses and drivers for their new business.

They haphazardly developed a business plan that included four buses and some of the top beachfront hotels and restaurants and coined it Palace Night Club Tours. They worked closely with the hotel concierges, restaurant managers, entertainment directors, and their drivers. They carefully paid attention to detail to ensure that their clients would be picked up from their hotels, taken to dinner, then to a club to see stellar entertainment before they were taken back to their hotels. They created a gorgeous brochure. They stocked the hotels with them. They went out their first evening with two busses, almost half-full. They were encouraged. They didn't expect to fill four buses the first night.

There was a problem, however. The Miami Beach City Council requested that an officer of the company attend the next day's meeting to ensure they had the proper permits to keep operating, or some such explanation. Neither my mother nor Ray wanted to attend the meeting, so they told me, "You have to participate because our license depends on it. We are too busy to take the time to attend."

I was terrified. Having never spoken in public before, I was now asked to go to the podium and speak in front of the Miami Beach City Council (which might as well have been the UN) and convince them to approve my mother and stepfather's license. I was only sixteen. It was crazy. They told me what to say, which was basically a handful of nonsensical sentences, and I did. And if they weren't interested in what I had to say and the business failed, would it be my fault? I walked away humiliated. The council paid little attention to me, they talked over me the entire time I was speaking and said they would let the company officers know of their decision shortly.

After this experience, I was never comfortable speaking in public again. As a public relations professional, I have been asked to speak at various agencies and client companies and I declined. Also, a friend who was a college professor teaching public relations and marketing asked me to speak to her class and I couldn't do it. I agreed to speak only once to a Los Angeles office of a national PR firm. It was awful. I was too loud. Too fast. Too nervous. Just the thought of doing it again scared and embarrassed me.

Two days later, the council made its decision. My mother and stepfather were officially out of business. Three buses were scheduled for that evening. They had to be cancelled. They had to refund deposits. Pay the drivers. Pay for the buses. They operated for one night. They lost all of the savings they invested, along with the considerable funds given to them by Oma and Opa. Just another Miami Beach nightmare.

Chapter 20

Anna & Arthur & Mia & Simon

At the same time that our new family of four was starting a new chapter in Miami Beach, my father was already a year into starting his new life 3,000 miles away from us in Southern California—virtually abandoning me and Simon. He moved to Tarzana, in the San Fernando Valley. In a very beautiful apartment. Why was it that he always had a nicer home? Better furniture? Better televisions? Better stereo equipment? It was night and day comparing the homes. My mother tried to make it as nice as she could, but it never looked as good as our father's home. That was hard to understand. His beautiful new apartment complex didn't allow children. But he smooth-talked them into allowing his children every summer.

He didn't move to Southern California alone. He asked Anna to marry him when she graduated college. She was thrilled. How else could she feel? She knew nothing else. They were married two days after she accepted her diploma. She was twenty-two and he was thirty-eight.

My nanny escaped the shame she would have felt for her youngest son, as she had passed away three years before in 1965.

My dad sexually abused Anna and forced her to grow up long before she was capable. And she didn't even know it. She was an immigrant in every negative connotation of the word, especially when she was a little girl. She couldn't speak "the language," "didn't know the rules," and had no money.

I wanted to go to their wedding and asked my mother if Simon and I could attend. I truly didn't understand that there was anything wrong with him marrying Anna. Anticipating that my mother would say that we could, I was prepared to ask if she would buy me a new dress for the occasion. Keeping pretty cool, my mother responded, "You and Simon cannot go to the wedding. Absolutely not." When I protested, she stormed out of the room hollering (and likely in tears), "Because I said so." It took me years to understand what I thought was a very unfair decision.

After they were married, our annual voyage out west began. We would spend two weeks of every summer with our father and Anna.

My father played it so cool, like it was a perfectly normal situation for your sister/cousin to become your stepmother. How fun. How fortuitous. We won't lose Anna now that she's all grown up. She'll just be our stepmother instead of our cousin. And daddy's new wife.

Since Anna had lived with us for nearly eight years, it wasn't strange or uncomfortable for Simon and me to spend time with her and our father. In fact, it barely registered that she had transitioned from being our sister to our stepmother. We were thrilled that she was back in our lives. It was when we arrived back home to our mother that we had to be especially careful not to talk about her, and for years we didn't really understand why. Nor did we understand the pain this marriage caused our mother. She would try and tell us, but it was never in a calm, soft-spoken manner. She was always very loud and defensive, shouting insults directed at my father and Anna, making us more confused.

While it's clear to me that Anna endured the most suffering by marrying my father, an enormous group of people in my dad's inner circle—Simon and me, our mother, my father's parents and my mother's parents—were also traumatized. There was also Anna's mother and stepfather. They didn't want Anna to marry my father. "Anna, he's too old. He was married to your cousin Rose. Aunt

Samantha's daughter. None of it is right." Irene didn't stand a chance. Anna was so brainwashed and so happy at that point that her mother knew she had two choices—stay in Anna's life or leave. Same as Arthur's mother. Both mothers stayed, while my father destroyed most everything he touched.

Chapter 21

Aunt Jean & Uncle Jerry & Rusty & Scott

Arthur's older brother, Jerry, and his wife, Jean, also lived in the San Fernando Valley. They lived in Encino, an affluent, gorgeous neighborhood. In fact, they bought the model home in their development when they first moved to California from New York with their two small sons. In 1959, Jerry was the president of a resort company in Santa Barbara. The company flew him by helicopter three times weekly to their headquarters in Santa Barbara. This was likely the time that my father's jealousy of his older brother started. And never ended.

He commented on Jerry's every move. It started out small. He often commented to me and Simon that their living room furniture was so "cheap and ugly" (it was actually quite expensive and beautiful). A rounded couch? A big metal starburst wall clock hanging nearby? A really busy carpet? His jealously graduated to bigger purchases every decade. His brother's choice in cars. A 1965 Lincoln Continental? In Huron Blue Metallic? "And what kind of a fancy ass color is that? It is an ugly dark blue."

But my father's favorite thing to mock his brother about was his height. And he did so, constantly. I always thought it was the only thing my father ever truly felt he had over Jerry, who was a fairly short 5'8", compared to his 5'11". And when my uncle Jerry's hair turned gray long before my father's—because he was much older— and he colored it very black, my dad constantly mocked him, telling us that our uncle colored his hair with "cheap shoe polish." It was

Mia McDaniel

a very long time before I realized he was making the shoe polish part up.

He continued to insult Jerry behind his back relentlessly, until 1996 when he suffered the first of two strokes. His brother and sister-in-law couldn't do enough to help him when he was down, even though they hadn't been speaking for years. They visited him when he was home from the hospital and had him over for lunch every week. He was down and out. And they were there. They were also there for me when I moved to Southern California in 1977, until they died. Aunt Jean in 1993 and Uncle Jerry in 2007. And my father knew how good they were to me and how much I adored them, but it didn't matter to him.

For two years before my father relocated and got settled in his new apartment with Anna, he took Simon and me to California for nearly two weeks in the summer, and we all stayed at Aunt Jean and Uncle Jerry's house with their sons, Rusty and Scott. Rusty and I were almost the same age, as were Simon and Scott. Oh, how I wished I'd had Rusty and Scott's life. Not only did their parents live together in a fabulous house, but they were kind to me and Simon. They took us places. We went to restaurants. The refrigerator and kitchen cupboards were stocked with amazing foods. And great snacks. Beef jerky. We had never heard of beef jerky. And lots of different potato and corn chips. And string cheese. And lemonade. Every day was a party in Encino.

Every year, we were treated to Disneyland, Universal Studios, the beach, Tijuana, clothes shopping, and plenty of eating out with Aunt Jean, Uncle Jerry, Rusty, and Scott. Now it was even more fun because Anna was with us too. Simon and I were always very well behaved because we didn't want to do anything that made our mother look bad. Simon and I knew better than to ever express our feelings about our new circumstances with our father. Instead, we focused on more trivial matters—should we go to Disneyland on Thursday or Friday?

Chapter 22

Mia & Simon & Arthur & Anna & Joanne

Tensions were always high at our mother's house, as she frequently expressed her disgust over our father's new marriage. We didn't understand what was disgusting about it, especially since our father repeatedly told us that he and Anna were much more compatible than he and our mother.

It was around this time, when I was seventeen that my father began to criticize me, and it seemed to me like it was all the time. Initially, he would question my fashion choices. My skirt was too long. My blouse was too frumpy. My skirt was too short. My blouse was too tight. One of his more hurtful insults was when he told me that I "looked like a slut" in the dark red lipstick I loved to wear as a teenager. Later in life, the hurt would go deeper. Questioning my allegiance to him. Questioning my lifestyle. Questioning my child-rearing.

In Tarzana, I had to be extremely careful not to say anything about my father or Anna that might upset him. Years later, I wondered if he was afraid that I would confront him about his relationship with Anna. But if he understood me at all, like a decent, caring father should have, he would have known that that was impossible. I had no clue as to what he put my cousin through. Or my mother. Or me and Simon for a very long time. No idea whatsoever.

I was discouraged from talking about my mother, unless it was to utter something objectionable. It was never okay to say that I missed my mother when we were in California. And I had to be careful not to want to call her too often. Tarzana with dad and Anna was a combination of entertainment, great food, new clothes, and criticism. Fortunately for Simon, he was rarely demeaned. He was a boy. He was too young. My father's disgraceful behavior haunted me my whole life.

Chapter 23

Mia & Wendy

As a sophomore at Miami Beach Senior High School, I met Wendy, who was a very pretty and petite fifteen-year-old with long brown locks and bushy eyebrows (that she somehow knew never to pluck). We became best friends very quickly. In fact, just months after meeting, it was Wendy's sixteenth birthday and her parents were throwing her a Sweet Sixteen birthday party. Her father, Victor, would become my surrogate father as I adored him. He owned a barbeque restaurant about twenty minutes away in Hallandale Beach and catered the party. Wendy was one of the popular girls and there must have been fifty kids at her party. I was thrilled to be invited. My days were so much better because of Wendy. We were inseparable.

I told Victor about my father and how he was of little to no influence on me and my brother's life. How he rarely called and just generally didn't seem interested in what was going on in our lives. And I told him about his marriage to Anna. I didn't put a negative spin on it because I still didn't recognize how reprehensible my father's behavior was. Victor, however, found my father's actions beyond comprehension and from that point on he was there for me anytime I needed fatherly support. He never tried to make my situation worse by calling out my dad, but instead was always available for counsel. Be it financial or emotional regarding my parents. Or really, anything else. I sent him Father's Day cards, to "Dad No. 2, in theory only," until he died in 1990.

$\sim$

Mia McDaniel

At the end of sophomore year, I met Dale who became my boyfriend for about a year. His family lived in a stunning house on Treasure Island, an expensive area about twenty minutes from my house. The most memorable thing for me about Dale's house was the formal living room that nobody sat in because the couches and big, stuffed chairs patterned in a wild zebra motif were covered in plastic.

Dale was sweet. And he was tall and good looking, which of course meant almost everything in high school. The biggest problem was that he wanted to have sex and I didn't. I just wanted to go to the Dunkin' Donuts that was across from the Venetian causeway where we could sit in the car, watch the boats, and eat donuts. It was a constant struggle, as high school relationships usually are centered around the ever-present "when are we going to do it?" Victor helped me. I was much more comfortable talking with him than my mother or stepfather.

"Honey, if you're not feeling like you are in love with him and don't want to have sex yet, or ever with him, stand your ground. I'm proud of you," he said.

"I'm really more scared than anything. I think I should be older and not this nervous and be in love. Thank you, Dad number two. Wendy is so lucky to have you."

Wendy knew she was lucky. The father and daughter adored each other. Though Wendy was so very tired of Victor's ongoing comments about the two of us, "Wendy, why can't you wear some makeup? Some lipstick? A pretty dress once in a while? Like Mia? Mia always looks so pretty, and you are just as pretty, even prettier, but you don't try."

"Because I have a different style. I don't like makeup, and I don't need lipstick," she told him. And she didn't.

However, when Wendy married her husband, Donald, in 1988, she donned a spectacular haute couture wedding gown, had her hair done in a beautiful chignon, and had her makeup applied by a professional. It was a stunning tribute to her father. Victor was glowing like a smiling jack-o'-lantern. Sadly, her mother, Sylvia, had died long before Wendy got married, passing in 1977.

∽

Miami Beach was very sad indeed in 1970. The hotels, that in the thirties, forties, and fifties were magnificent art deco masterpieces, were just old and tired. There were rows of beach chairs in front of every hotel where the senior retirees, who flew or drove down south for their vacations, would sit. And sit. And sit. And they made friends with other retirees who lived in Miami Beach and sometimes they would sit and sit and sit with them. And the shops they frequented were the same shops I went to. It was very depressing.

While I lived on the opposite end of the beachfront hotels on Collins Avenue, on Bay Road, it was still my neighborhood. We lived in South Beach. I sometimes shopped at the Thrifty's supermarket. The Collins fish market and Butterflake Bakery, where I loved surprising my oma and opa, my brother, mother, and Ray with delicious cakes and pastries. Dale and I went to the old, run-down movie theaters on Washington Avenue, where we saw double-features that were usually fifteen to twenty years old for thirty-five cents each. If you didn't mind the occasional cockroach...

Not all of Miami Beach, however, looked like Lummus Park did in the seventies—filled with seniors and their bright white zinc oxide face lotions—lying in the sun.[1]

There were plenty of young people in other neighborhoods. Neighborhoods where most of the Beach High students lived. And many lived in gorgeous mansions on Alton Road, Bay Road, and farther north in Golden Beach, where Wendy lived. I'll never forget going to a classmate's house and asking for the bathroom.

1 An incredible photography book, *Miami Beach*, photographed by two Miami Beach natives and Beach High alumni, Andy Sweet and Gary Monroe, is a stunning book published in 1990 that chronicles the city and its elderly population from 1977–1984. The photographs have been exhibited in art galleries and museums, and a Netflix documentary entitled The Last Resort is a stunning celebration of some of Miami's greatest artists, featuring their photos.

Mia McDaniel

He told me where "the ladies powder room" was. I started laughing and he gave me an odd stare. When I came out of this fabulous bathroom, I saw that there was another bathroom for the men. Then, my friend showed me most of the house, not including the wing they didn't use. I saw the gorgeous rooms facing the bay and had never seen anything comparable until I moved to Los Angeles.

Chapter 24
Simon

When I started Beach High in tenth grade, Simon was in fifth grade at Ida M. Fisher Junior High School. Today, we marvel at how well Simon survived his unsupervised childhood. At eleven, twelve, thirteen, and fourteen, he had little to no parental supervision. Our stepfather, Ray, was not much of a father figure and was married to our mother for just two years. Our father was 3,000 miles away and rarely called, and our mother was working. And uninterested. And trying to salvage her marriage. Opa tried his best to bond with him, and it helped, but it was never a stellar relationship.

Simon met his best friend David in sixth grade, and his family became more of a "real" family to him than ours. He was on their boat, at their house, or with David at the Baskin-Robbins on Lincoln Road where Simon worked when he was sixteen. And used the ice cream scales to weigh the weed he sold in the back of the store. He smoked pot for the first time at thirteen and began selling it at sixteen. He was too young. Why did he do that? Because he could, with little to no parental supervision. And there was also peer pressure among such young kids at that time.

When David was in ninth grade, he and his parents and brother sailed to the Bahamas, as they did often. They took a small plane ride around the islands, as they also did frequently. This time, the plane crashed. The whole family was killed, except for David's sister, who had stayed behind. Simon and I were devastated. It dominated local news that evening. It was horrendous.

Losing his best friend at twelve was one of the saddest things either of us had ever experienced. I have no recollection of my parents consoling him other than a brief, "So sorry, Simon." It was especially traumatic for him, not just because he lost David, but also David's family, who filled a huge void left unfulfilled by his own family. So many weekends spent with the Martins on their boat or at their house.

Simon went places that he shouldn't have because they were too far or too dangerous. He would take the bus from our home in South Miami Beach to Flagler Street in Miami, usually by himself. Not a place for a young kid to be alone. Often in dark movie theaters. And even when he was in a crowd—like the Pop Warner League (similar to Little League for football) in sixth grade—he was alone. Our mother never attended a football game. And when he played in The Miami Beach High Rock Ensemble, she wasn't there either. I wasn't there because I didn't know we were welcome.

But my brother and I did enjoy spending time at the beach together when I was in high school. We walked to Lincoln Road, took the tram to Washington Avenue, and walked to the beach. Sometimes we persuaded our mom to drop us off on the weekends. And sometimes pick us up. It was a bummer leaving the beach and schlepping back home with wet, sandy bathing suits, sticky suntan lotion, and beach towels. And my transistor radio. And some snacks, if we didn't finish them. We swam and sunbathed and talked. The conversations weren't too heavy since Simon was only eleven. But we talked. About school. And music. And our mother and father. And our stepmother/sister/cousin and stepfather. It wasn't until we were much older that we really talked about the hell we went through when our father blew up the family.

I think Simon became quite the entrepreneur at ten and a half years old, with a thriving little shoe-shine business because he somehow knew he would have to grow up fast. He knew our parents were not like other parents. I was so proud of him.

Simon had few disagreements with Ray, but he clearly remembers one altercation, completely unprovoked, in which Ray smacked him across the face. He literally "saw stars" and spun around. He was stunned. Ray did not apologize. Not then. Not ever. After that, Simon felt in his bones that there was "something not right" about his stepfather, and he didn't care that he lived in the same house. For him, Ray was now "out of the picture," he told me years later.

That's when he started to connect in a much deeper way with Benny from the local gas station. Benny had a heart of gold, and he shared it with Simon every single weekend. He saw that my little brother was a loner and could use a father figure. He quickly filled that void by hiring him to pump gas on the weekends. He picked Simon up at 7:00 a.m. every Saturday and Sunday and took him to a local restaurant for a breakfast of eggs and grits. For lunch, Benny and Simon went to the A&P where Benny bought white bread, ham, and Pepsis to eat back at the station. Benny talked to Simon. About school. About girls. About the gas station. He taught him how to do an oil change. Benny's influence and commitment to Simon, along with his posture as a role model, helped Simon grow up. And his childhood was considerably better because of Benny.

Simon felt like he was a kid in need of a father, but Ray was not ever going to be that father. He told me years later that he was forced to ride with Ray on his bus route, rather than stay at home alone after school (even though my grandparents were usually home, one floor below). He sat in the front seat of the bus and schlepped with Ray from South Miami Beach to Ft. Lauderdale several times a week—it was the most unpleasant task Simon had to do.

At thirteen, Simon bought a bass guitar using his bar mitzvah money (that was all he was able to buy as our mother took the rest and it was never mentioned again). He knew how to play the violin and had wanted to play the bass at eleven, but he was too short for the upright bass, so he learned the cello first. In spite of all these lessons at school, it seemed that our parents were mostly unaware of Simon's passion for music. When he planned to buy the bass, our mother implored him, "Why don't you buy a *real* guitar, one that you can bring to the beach and play for the girls."

And then, when Simon was a little older (fifteen to be exact) he thought he might have a chance to have sex for the first time with the beautiful daughter of our mother's best friend from Lefrak City. She was now an "older woman" at seventeen.

He went to her house in northern Florida where they had been living for a few years. It was about a six-hour drive from Miami Beach. Apparently a male friend of mine drove him there and back and never told me. She was home alone. They were very happy to see each other and before too long, they went to bed. Simon lost his virginity. With his mother's best friend's daughter. And she lost her virginity to Simon.

When she miscalculated and didn't get her period the following month, all hell broke loose. She told her mother. Her mother told my mother.

My mother told Arthur. And the disgusting, immature man who was our father, congratulated Simon, "Good job. Not too smart with your mother's best friend's daughter though," he said. If I had been in Simon's shoes, my father would have called me a slut and humiliated me. For a boy, it was different. He was commended. The love and respect my father demonstrated for boys and the lack thereof for girls would evolve into the same destructive behavior with men and women. Anna was the first casualty. And I was the second.

Simon was mostly a loner, but he did make a few very close friends including Martin, who is still a friend today. Martin and Simon drove to Los Angeles in 1976, when Simon graduated Beach High early in order to be a California resident before he was eighteen so he could attend Berkeley at the cheaper in-state tuition. He missed the final Rock Ensemble show and the prom, but Arthur didn't have to pay exorbitant rates for college.

At seventeen, just before moving out West, he made another best friend, also named Simon. They were very close and remained friends when Simon moved to Coral Gables and attended a different high school. Shortly after moving to California, his friend Simon got a motorcycle and rode too fast near his home. He crashed and died. On Mother's Day.

My little brother. No one should have to experience so much death and suffering, especially a child. When this happened, Simon was in California and I was still in Miami Beach, so I wasn't able to console him during this difficult time.

Simon planned to fly to Miami Beach for the funeral. Our father said, "That's asinine. Do you know how expensive that is? And to be there, for what, two nights? They can't get on without you?" Simon couldn't respond. He walked away. Of course it was necessary that he be there. My little brother was a source of much love to the family, and they likewise helped him get through the horrendous accident. To not join them in their unspeakable grief was not even a remote possibility. Once again, our callous father showed his lack of compassion. Today, Simon is still very close with Simon's sister.

Chapter 25
Mia

Like most teens, I had a summer job, working at the local Publix grocery store a few blocks from home. I worked in between daily sunbathing with the familiar 11"x14" aluminum sheet and iodine for the inevitable super, super sunburn before it peeled to reveal a golden bronze tan.

The store was not only a way to make money but also a true source of entertainment. The girls were cashiers and many became my friends. Many of the boys were bag boys, and I dated some of them, as well as Michael, the assistant produce manager. He was twenty when I was seventeen, and he escorted me to Beach High's senior prom. Michael had turned down four girls in previous years and I still wonder where I got the confidence to ask him.

The boys were sweet and attractive and there were two in particular that liked me. And I liked them. It was 1970 when one of them, Enrique, was bagging for me, and I remembered that I needed to buy Kotex napkins before I went home that evening. At that time, the boxes were enormous. As big as a giant box of knee-high boots. I quietly and very discreetly asked one of my very first Cuban friends, Yolanda, who was married and wouldn't be embarrassed, if she could buy the box for me and give it to me at the end of our shift. Outside. Alone. By my car. Yolanda said that of course she would and she understood. I paid her for the box and forgot all about it, checking customers and talking with Enrique. Until...Yolanda hollered from the dreaded aisle, "Mia, regular or super?" I was horrified and wished the floor could have opened up and swallowed me as Enrique burst out laughing.

David, who became a Miami Beach firefighter, was another boy at Publix I liked and he became a dear friend. He accompanied me on a few occasions to visit my opa in the Miami Heart Institute where Opa died in 1974. David and I got together again in the early 2000s when he would once again come to a hospital, this time to see my mother when she was first diagnosed with emphysema.

While working at Publix, I became friends with a new girl who moved across the street from our house on Bay Road. Her name was Gail and years later she would become the casting director for a major motion picture studio in Los Angeles. We became as inseparable as Wendy and I were years earlier. And Gail got a job at Publix too. We arrived together and left together. Gail was also dating Pedro, one of the dreamy Cubans. Life was fun when I was working and playing with Gail. Walking around Miami Beach with a thermos of white Russians and a couple of joints: one black, one pink. Our "Good & Plenty's." We reconnected in the early eighties when I saw Gail's name as casting director of a big-budget Hollywood movie. We lost touch and then connected again when my daughter wanted to become an actress, and I asked Gail to arrange some auditions. She did, and I was grateful. I even set Gail up with my ex-husband's best friend George and once with my good friend Arnie. But eventually our friendship just fizzled. Gail confessed to being quite the loner.

Chapter 26

Ben

I met the first love of my life when I was nearly nineteen and a freshman at Miami Dade Junior College. His name was Ben. His father was Benny, who owned the gas station, and had developed that wonderful bond with Simon a few months before. Ben occasionally helped his dad at the station, which was only a few blocks from our house. He was the handsomest man I'd ever met. He wasn't especially tall, maybe 5'10", but he had a stunning build. Gorgeous smile. Beautiful brown eyes. He worked out with weights before anyone other than Jack LaLanne worked out with weights. And he blow-dried his hair. Ben noticed me coming in to get gas in my little blue car and asked if I would like to go to the beach the following weekend. I told him I would like that and I was so excited. But so terrified. Not only was he a doll, but he was twenty-two. I'd never been out with anyone older than my prom date who was twenty. And I was still eighteen.

He picked me up, and I was wearing the biggest, longest cover-up on top of the biggest, longest, drapiest bathing suit I could find. He gently chided me with something like, "Really?" He had a dune buggy and we rode along the beach, swam, and went out for a long lunch. I had the best date ever. He wanted to see me again. He took me to the Red Lobster for dinner the following weekend. It was wonderful. I loved being with him. I kissed him goodbye or goodnight after every date. We went out for about three months, and he wanted to take me to bed. I was a virgin. And I was very scared.

He didn't know I was a virgin. It didn't come up and I didn't see a need to announce it.

But when I finally agreed to have sex with him, I told him first that I was a virgin. He was shocked and initially wanted to take me right home. But I convinced him, "I'm so ready and excited for you to be my first lover." I loved him. And he seemed to love me, though I always felt he was hiding something. We had unprotected sex (for the only time in my life as a single woman) and the next week one of my best friends took me to a doctor to get birth control pills.

Ben and I went out every weekend, and I couldn't wait for him to take me home. I couldn't spend the night because I was living at home, saving money to move out. But earlier, when I went to the University of Florida in Gainesville about six hours away, I would frequently come home, not let my mother know, and stay with Ben. It was heaven.

I knew Ben had been in the Marines. In fact, when I moved to California, he gave me his Marines tie clip as a romantic gesture. I knew he graduated college, but I didn't know from where. And I didn't care. I also knew that he and his former girlfriend had robbed a bank. Yes, they robbed a bank. His ex-girlfriend worked at a nearby bank as a teller. It was 1967. Somehow she was able to steal about $10,000 and they flew to Hawaii. The only reason they were caught was because while driving their rental car in Honolulu, they were stopped for speeding. Court cases ensued, and for a technicality that I never understood, they were not convicted.

Ben loved Sharon, not his previous girlfriend who robbed the bank, but his beloved married girlfriend whom he wasn't going to give up. They had met three years before he met me, and he saw her whenever *she* could see him. It wasn't often and didn't really get in the way of our plans, but she got in the way of our relationship. How could she not? They also had a son together. She lived with her husband on Fisher Island, a barrier island three miles offshore of mainland South Florida, with the highest per capita income

Mia McDaniel

anywhere in the United States. When I asked Ben how they knew for sure that the little boy was his and not Sharon's husband's, he showed me a photograph. His toes were webbed, just like Ben's.

Now, one would think a nice Jewish girl from Miami Beach, who was a virgin until she was nineteen, almost never drank and didn't do drugs, rarely smoked pot, would dump a guy who was a bank robber, had an ongoing three-year relationship with his married girlfriend, and had his very own son. Nope. Our romance lasted nearly four years, including long-distance when I was in college.

My romance with Ben can probably be attributed to several factors, mostly leading back to my mother and, particularly, my father. There didn't seem to be many boundaries for my parents. I observed my mother dating married men and didn't understand that it wasn't acceptable behavior. I didn't know it was scandalous for my father to marry Anna. And when my mother was married to Ray, I was forced to lie to the police when they entered our house looking for him.

The primary rationality, however, was that Ben treated me so well. I didn't have a father or a mother to really look up to and teach me about love and relationships. Ben was kind. He was a gentleman. He wouldn't let me pay for anything. He made me so happy. I made him happy, too, even though apparently I wasn't enough.

I also was afraid that I couldn't possibly fall in love with someone the way I fell in love with him. He flew to Manhattan Beach in 1978 when I first moved there. I was involved with someone else at the time but was willing to jeopardize that relationship to spend a week with Ben. (The man I was seeing would never speak to me again.) Ben took me to Lake Tahoe where he always dreamed of building an "A-frame" house, the ubiquitous architecture that wealthy homeowners built there. I often wondered if maybe I would live there with him. Would we be married? Would we have children? He couldn't stay with married Sharon forever, could he? I knew his affluent girlfriend showered him with gifts. Expensive, luxurious gifts. He wore a stunning Piaget watch (not that I had ever heard of that luxury brand). He had cashmere sweaters for the cool evenings in the fall and winter at the beach. He had a beautiful leather toiletry bag engraved with his name that he brought to California. And more.

My mother always commented on how gorgeous Ben was and how "lucky" I was to be dating such a handsome and kind man. Excuse me, but shouldn't a mom think the man who was dating her daughter was the lucky one? It hurt my feelings and didn't help my self-confidence. My mother also went on about how Ben's father, Benny, was very good looking, as well. In fact, at forty-eight, he was almost as handsome as his son. I supposed that must have been why my mother started *dating* my boyfriend's father. My boyfriend's *married* father. How fucked up is that? Who does that to her own daughter? Even if Benny were single, it was bound to be awkward. But married? I was always uncomfortable that my mother went out with Benny. I didn't find it "cute" like she did. I found it extremely unsettling.

Ben and I eventually broke up because it just wasn't geographically desirable and because he wanted me to have more than a boyfriend devoted to his married girlfriend and son. He wanted me to date college boys. He wanted me to excel in my studies. He was proud of me. He even said he was "thrilled and honored" that he took my virginity. But he said I had to move on. I thought I'd never get over it. And Wendy was out of the country in England with many of our friends at a university overseas transfer program for six months. (My father said I didn't need to go abroad. I could learn plenty staying in Gainesville.) And I wouldn't think of turning to either one of my parents for comfort. They'd never been my "go-to."

Chapter 27
Mia

Finally, I stopped crying and realized that I was not going to spend my life with Ben. I wanted to date again and get a boyfriend. I was behaving just like my mother after she divorced my father, wanting more than anything to have a boyfriend, or in her case, a husband. The time I spent in college would be the most miserable time in my life. Not the academic part. I loved journalism. And advertising. And public relations. But I had no parental support system. Not then. Not ever. I had no confidence. I was just sad deep inside to my core. I looked happy. Smiled. Wore lipstick and nail polish, which wasn't all that popular among hippies in the mid-seventies. I wore perfume. I started sleeping around, like everyone else. It was the seventies. It was the time of love, sex, and rock and roll. I was supposed to be loving all this loving.

But I wasn't. It was heart-breaking. I was promiscuous. And everyone around me was too, but they were so damned happy. I wasn't enjoying myself. Being available to men, thinking it would eventually lead to a boyfriend and ultimately a husband, was flawed thinking. I was trying to fill a void of loneliness for male attention, in which my father was mostly responsible. But it didn't work, especially when I was so distraught the day after a one-night stand, which happened more than once. I remember one time when I was renting an apartment with another college student. It was a fairly new living situation for me: a two-bedroom place only about five minutes from Wendy and her boyfriend. My roommate seemed okay, but I never tried to befriend her. I was embarrassed by my many dates, and she had a steady boyfriend. I was so afraid that she was judging me. I remember one morning, coming back to my room, trying to appear invisible after leaving a boy's house and feeling so ashamed and sad and just not knowing what to do to be happy. I would see the yellow, red, and green tapestry that I used as a blanket on my bed in the dark room and collapse into it. I could have stayed there for days weeping.

As an adult, I often wondered why I didn't say anything to my parents during so many lonely times as a kid, as a college student, as an adult in my twenties, and as a young mother in my thirties, who desperately wanted and needed her family. I didn't ask for any help, as a child or a young mother. I didn't complain that they were never available. I didn't expect my mother or father to be available. To offer parental support. I knew better than to question their actions. I knew this at a very young age. My parents always came first. Always before me and Simon. I felt my parents' love was conditional. They regularly uttered the words, "I love you, Mia," and I wanted to believe they did and would eventually really prove it.

I became very needy as an adult. As a very young and immature college girl (emotionally much younger than my nineteen years), I didn't know how to relax and make friends with boys. I didn't give myself or the boys a chance. If he was good looking and intelligent, I was laser-focused on developing a romantic relationship with him almost from the moment we met. It took me years to understand that the lonely and sad relationships I formed with men, particularly in my early twenties, was the result of my pitiful relationship with my father. He was never there for me, and never a role model for me of a good father, or even a good man. He never protected me and the consequences of a nonexistent fatherly bond were so much worse because he was physically in my life. He hadn't died.

I called him every few weeks to check in and there were times when I needed more help with my expenses. Even though I worked throughout college, expenses were often difficult to handle without any help. I only asked for assistance with utility bills, textbooks, and clothing necessities, not fancy handbags, designer makeup, or leather boots. One time, we had an enormous argument when I told him I needed new shoes. The university campus was quite large, and I did a lot of walking. He told me he wouldn't help me. He insisted that he had done enough. "Figure it out," he said. When I hung up the phone, I was crying. It was about more than new shoes. It was about how he treated his only daughter. A friend that Wendy and I knew from high school dropped by and when I opened my bedroom door, I heard him ask Wendy if I just got off the phone with my dad because he heard me crying. My friends came to expect that. I could always count on my father to put me through unnecessary anxiety and heartache whenever we spoke.

My parents didn't even drive me to school when I started college. When each of my children went off to college, it was a huge deal for the whole family, as we all flew back east and stayed for a week. But not Rose and Arthur. My father was in California, but my mother was only six hours away in Miami Beach with me and Simon. One of my close friends, Yvonne, drove me to the campus about six hours away. My heart was heavy and so envious of the families dropping off their kids to begin this exciting chapter. I got to my dorm room and cried.

When I met my roommate, I cried again. We stayed out of each other's way and never had a friendship. I was too immature to accept my situation and got a family physician friend to help me vacate the dorm because of "a medical condition."

When I became a mother, however, the lack of lessons from my parents resulted in a plethora of lessons for my own children. They came first. As did my husband. They often complained that their mom was too protective.

In college, I mostly kept to myself how sad and insecure I was. Wendy told me years later that she always thought I loved my college life. The boys. I was so popular. Had so many friends. And lovers too.

She was stunned when I gave her the backstory about how miserable I had felt.

I got excellent grades. I smoked pot. I had an occasional Southern Comfort or a glass of Blue Nun or Lancers wine (the best of the cheapest wines at the time). At least we could afford to drink better wines than Boone's Farm. And Wendy and I never ate Hamburger Helper without the hamburger like some of our friends did. I also gingerly experimented with the newest drugs, with only my best buddies. I dropped Windowpane (LSD) and Orange Sunshine (LSD) once and snorted cocaine a couple of times. But I didn't get stoned before class. My grades throughout college were mostly A's with some B's, except for the required political science and economics courses that I was thrilled to get a "C" and "D" in respectively.

The drug experimentation was a confluence of several things for me. For one, it was the mid-seventies and the University of Florida had a flourishing drug culture and I was a hippie, as were most of my friends. I didn't date fraternity boys, though that was more about not feeling "good enough" for those boys than not wanting to date them. Also, my father did not hide his pot smoking from his kids. While initially he didn't encourage us to smoke pot with him, he flaunted how hip and trendy he was, letting us believe that marijuana was perfectly safe and risk-free. However, years later I didn't know whether to be proud or ashamed of him when I was at a small dinner party at the house of a man I was dating. We were seated at the dining room table and I saw a beautiful platter on a side table with business cards on it. And whose card was on top? Arthur Weinberg's. My father. I was shocked and asked my date, "Why do you have my father's business card?" He told me my father sold them weed. I didn't respond and wondered what the partygoers thought of me. And of my father. I was very confused and upset. I told Simon, but not my father.

I still tried to convince myself that he was the youngest, hippest, coolest father around. Another reason to let his narcissism and bad behavior slide was me still wanting as much attention as I could get from him.

Unlike every single one of my friends, then and now, I couldn't wait to be done with college. I had career goals. I had no self-esteem. No self-love. No self-confidence in anything. Except in my chosen profession. And I would feel that way about myself for years. Until I married my first husband in 1983, before it went bad.

My jobs throughout school were mostly secretarial jobs, including my favorite for the chair of the Broadcasting Department in the College of Journalism and Communications, where I attended most of my classes. I also worked in the school's teaching hospital as a secretary and in the Agriculture Department as a secretary. The positions were always short-term, though. I was looking for a new part-time job when one of the advertising professor's assistants told me about a job with Domino's Pizza. We were doing some mockup ads on Domino's in class, and he knew of an opening at the warehouse where the pepperoni, onions, green peppers, and cheese were prepared for the pizzas. Sounded great. And this was years before I became a vegetarian. I loved pepperoni. I took the job only to find out that it was in an industrial park. And I was the only one there. It was very dark. Nobody around. Big warehouse. My little blue Toyota by itself in the parking lot. At night.

I needed the money and this time I couldn't find another secretarial position at the school. My shift was 5:00 p.m. to 9:00 p.m., five nights a week. It was frightening. I locked the giant steel doors, turned on my transistor radio, and sliced. And sliced. And sliced. And helped myself to some pepperoni, cheese, and peppers. I told my dad about the job, and that I was very uncomfortable in that setting. Even a little scared. But there weren't any other jobs that I could find.

The struggles I had with him over money defied explanation. He could afford it. I was working and got excellent grades. Instead of being supportive and kind, he told me, "You need to toughen up. It won't hurt you. Lock the door. Grow up."

I was a nervous wreck every evening that I worked there, and as soon as I could, I got another secretarial gig at the university. It took about four months. I never talked to my father about it again. And the refrigerator at the house I shared with Wendy and three other girlfriends was fairly well stocked with pepperonis and green peppers. I even heard the jingle that I wrote in my advertising copywriting class on the radio as Domino's local Christmas ad. I didn't pursue payment and they didn't offer it up. They paid me in pepperoni.

Chapter 28

Mia

After graduating the University of Florida in 1975 with a BS in Advertising that I found rather ironic, and somewhat hilarious, I lived by myself in North Miami Beach. It was the first time I had lived alone, and it was wonderful because I had a good job and was making new friends. I knew I wanted a career in advertising. Or journalism. Or public relations. I also knew that I desperately wanted to work for a television station and was fortunate to find an opening at WCIX, Channel 6, an independent Miami TV station. The job was as a secretary in the credit department. I had absolutely no qualms about being employed in the highly unglamorous credit department. I just wanted to have a job at the station, where I planned to move up the ladder. It was a two-person department. Just me and my enormous, flirtatious, unattractive Cuban boss. I worked with him for about six months until I couldn't deal with his obnoxious flirting any longer. He crossed the line when he said, "If you go with me on my next business trip, I can make sure you get a promotion and a bigger salary, if you know what I mean." That sent me to the general manager's (GM) office, where his wonderful, supportive secretary told the GM, and I was transferred the following week to the advertising sales department.

Years later—predating the "Me Too" movement—I was very proud of myself for calling attention to this man rather than submitting (which I knew I never would) or ignoring him. Or turning him down and trying to keep my job. Though there were times

I questioned myself and my integrity and wondered if I would have been more agreeable if he was a better-looking "potential husband." I like to think not.

I loved my job and I flourished. I even auditioned for a local television program on the sixth-floor studio of the famed round building. When the candidate was chosen and it wasn't me, the GM told me that he reviewed the tape and thought I was very good. I was one of the top five candidates, and he said he wanted to talk with me should there be any other opportunities.

I thought little of it and retreated to my dark place of low self-esteem, little confidence, and just plain sadness. I assumed he only told me that to keep me working there. And my mother offered me no understanding or compassion. Contrarily, she chided me for thinking it was even possible. I didn't speak with the GM again. I stayed at the station for another six months, hoping to find another position quickly so I wouldn't have to be reminded of what I labeled "a failure" rather than an opportunity.

I moved to a small advertising agency on Lincoln Road in Miami Beach. It was 1976 and I had plans to move to California by 1980. My father lived there, with Joanne, wife number three, and we were getting along just fine (undoubtedly because I didn't ask for anything from him). More importantly, Simon lived there and would soon attend the University of California, Berkeley, majoring in political science. And would soon opine on every presidential candidate, every gubernatorial candidate, nearly anything of any significance when it came to politics in California, the United States, and the world. At Berkeley, my dear, sweet little brother would continue to pursue his love of music. Following his two years with the Miami Beach High School Rock Ensemble, he would play the upright bass in the Berkeley Jazz Band. And with the Jazz Band, he would tour Japan. He would live in Japan for one year, in Hong Kong for two years, and in England for a year. And tour the world, which became his biggest love. Today, he has his own jazz recording label and has won five Grammys. I've often thought that his path to survival was just leaving. Traveling. Staying far away from our parents for as long as he could. I'm not even sure it was a conscious choice.

In 1997, he married Danielle, whom he met in Paris and then she became his biggest love. After nearly thirteen years, they divorced and then his girlfriend Sophia became his wife and his biggest love and still is today. His father's impact on his life was marginally better than it was on mine, simply because he was male and because he was usually in another country. Our father and mother constantly complained to me about his traveling. They couldn't understand why he would want to visit faraway, beautiful places instead of getting "a real job." They were mean, not wanting to understand, but rather wanting to complain. While I didn't want his lifestyle, I always admired his chutzpah and love of travel.

In 2000, when Simon was already successful in the music industry for many years, he got his master's degree as a marriage and family therapist. I often wondered if he chose that path as a coping mechanism to deal with his own issues with our father or because he succeeded, albeit briefly, each time he tried to bring his father and sister together.

Chapter 29

Mia's Best Friend Michael

It was 1977 and my very best friend in the whole wide world was and always will be Michael. We met at the advertising agency where we both worked in downtown Los Angeles, when I lived in Manhattan Beach and Michael lived in the mid-Wilshire area.

Michael. He was tall, dark, and handsome. Kind, sweet, and wonderful. And smart. When we met, he was twenty-seven and I was twenty-three. The best friend ever. And, I had pretty much refused to accept that this wonderful, gorgeous, sweet, single, Jewish man was gay. Even after visiting his beautiful home in Los Angeles that he shared with his boyfriend, Dick. The home had two bedrooms. Only one had a bed in it. A king-size bed. The other had a few chairs and fabulous drapes. Not wanting to embarrass his new friend, Michael told me that they were "still decorating" the second bedroom, even though they had lived in the house for two years. Finally, months later, and after countless discussions, Michael begged my friend Anita to explain to me that he adored me, but a romance wasn't in our future because he was gay. He saw an enduring, amazing friendship. But not a sexual relationship or marriage.

I was so sad, but reluctantly accepted that Michael would never be my boyfriend. Or husband. But he would be my very best friend always and my soulmate.

It was the best relationship I would ever have with a man that wasn't romantic. And the most enduring, beautiful friendship. And, of course, he was "my backup." If I wasn't married and pregnant by thirty-five, he would be willing to impregnate me. This meant we would have to have sex, as there was no IVF at the time. While I knew this wasn't something Michael especially wanted to do, (I didn't either anymore) he would do anything for me. And it was mutual.

In 1989, Michael died of AIDS, at only thirty-nine. He made a giant impression on me. I absolutely adored him. There wasn't anything we couldn't and didn't talk about. We were so close for the twelve short years we shared. At his memorial, that he desperately insisted be called "a party," Michael's parents; brother; sister; boyfriend, Dick; and his best friend, me, spoke as per his instructions written in the private letter he sent each of us just weeks before he died.

How amazing that he had the presence of mind to write this letter and make sure everyone he wanted to speak, or attend, received it. And Dick had arranged for Marianne Williamson to speak at the beginning and the end of the ceremony. She privately told me right before she went home, "Unfortunately, I'm going to more and more of these terribly sad events and there is always one woman who is clearly the most special woman in the world to the man who died of AIDS. I can see that that woman is you." I was so touched and cried again after Marianne said that. It meant so much to me. I was that woman and was devastated that my darling Michael had succumbed to a cruel, fatal illness. But I was surrounded by love at Michael's party. My best friends knew Michael, and they all came to the celebration of his life and watched out for me all day. We had a videographer and every few years I try to watch the tape.

In his letter, Michael identified the relationship he had with each person he loved—and tagged me as his soulmate. The night he died, I dreamed he was with me pointing to the sole of his shoe and smiling an enormous, gorgeous smile. It was my first of many "visits" from Michael.

I felt the same way about him and remained friends with his mother and father until their deaths many years later. And his sister, who passed almost exactly ten years to the day after he did.

And I loved the beautiful AIDS quilt that his parents had made for him, to be part of the incredible touring exhibition of AIDS quilts. They traveled to a few cities to see it and sent me photographs. It amazed me how his mother and father were able to find and work with a designer and quilter while experiencing unimaginable grief.

Today, my family and I are still very close to Arnie, Michael's younger brother and the only family member left. I named my second child for my exquisite friend, Michael. And I told Sam and Michael before they went to college that Michael had left each of them "a little seed money" to be used for their education. Sam and Michael spent their inheritance on books, school supplies, and a splash of dorm décor.

Chapter 30
Anna & Arthur & Joanne

My father unceremoniously dumped Anna in 1972 after four years of marriage and nearly fourteen years of abuse and playing house with her. He wasn't kind when he brutishly told Anna that it was simply over. He wanted out. She was only twenty-six. She was devastated. He stole her childhood. Her teenage years. Her early adulthood. And he was no longer interested. She knew the real reason was because he couldn't control her the way he used to. "I outgrew my place for him. After four years, he wanted a divorce. He couldn't manipulate me so totally anymore," she told me in 2005.

She continued, "The straw that broke the camel's back was one night when I wanted to go out with some girlfriends. He didn't want me to. Not for any particular reason, he just didn't want me to leave him alone. I grabbed my car keys, and he tried to wrestle them from me. And he was successful. I see it so vividly, as if it was yesterday. Everything changed the next day.

"He went on 'business trips' all the time. He was never home. God knows what he really did. He kept telling me, though, that he was faithful. I wasn't sure why. I believed him but it didn't matter. He was done. I was showing him that I had a mind of my own. And he did have a God complex. He was in charge of everything. Who was I to disobey him? To question him?"

Anna and my father lived in a beautiful home in West Hills, and Simon and I loved being there. They had a swimming pool and a big, beautiful kitchen with a large pantry that they stocked with delicious snacks for us. And they had Shamus, a huge and playful Alaskan Malamute puppy. I remember feeling so badly for Anna when my father told me that they were getting divorced. I remember he was flippant about it—he just explained that it had run its course and it was over.

I was very surprised and when Anna provided details years later, I was horrified. She said it felt like he discarded her like yesterday's trash.

She went on to tell me, "He put the house up for sale right away. I was twenty-six. I didn't know I was entitled to half the house. I didn't know shit. I got nothing except for an ancient Volkswagen Beetle, while he took the gorgeous, brand-new Buick Skylark convertible. If he could have driven two cars at the same time, I likely wouldn't have even gotten that. I was unworldly and had spent the last thirteen to fourteen years of my life with this man. I thought he was my protector. He was everything to me. For the first time in my life, I was all alone. For the first time in half of my life, I was without him. I could hardly imagine my life without your father. And I had no money and no place to live. I was broken."

Not my father though. He was moving on and looking to replace Anna. He dated and was very content with his new status, but when he was offered a position in Philadelphia, he was excited to be a single man in a whole new place. On the East Coast, again. Within a few months, he met Joanne, a high school English teacher. They lived in the same building of a beautiful apartment complex, about ten miles east of downtown. At first, he wondered why she'd never been married. After all, she was twenty-nine (not exactly an "old maid" but maybe on the cusp in 1975). They dated and the story goes that they rather quickly fell in love (though I don't believe my father knew how to love) and married. We were not invited to our father's wedding.

Joanne was unlike anyone I had ever known, and hopefully, I will never, ever know anyone like her again. In the beginning, she

Mia McDaniel

befriended me. I was her husband's daughter, after all, and it didn't seem like much of a burden to be nice to me. We laughed a lot. We shared dinner every evening with my father when I lived with them for a few months when I first moved to California. We grocery shopped together. We went to movies. We went to lunch. But she had a different, deviant reason for being nice at first.

She set out to poison my relationship with my father and nobody was more surprised than me. It took Joanne years of strategized, hard work to accomplish that. But she did. Not that he was blameless, but as big of a bully as he was, he didn't argue much with Joanne when it came to his children. Or most anything else. I was powerless against her deceit and his support of her. When he suffered his first of two massive strokes in 1996, he was defenseless. Joanne was one of the premier real estate brokers in Beverly Hills, and my father was one of the premier business brokers there, and she felt compelled to support him when he could no longer work.

Joanne supporting our dad, with a good deal of assistance from me and Simon, was a huge relief financially. But she made it hell in every other way. She felt she owned him. The reason why she did this is a mystery. He even had a new fiancée, Joyce. Joanne would keep up this charade that the couple never divorced for the rest of my father's life, claiming they were married for forty-five-plus years, when they were actually married for only fourteen. When he died, the only thing I wanted was his college ring that he wore every day of his life. I remembered being a child at his college graduation. I likely wouldn't even wear it. I just wanted to have it for when I wanted to look at it. Joanne told Simon to tell me that she wasn't going to give me his ring, even though she didn't want it. She was his executor.

I often wondered why Joanne would ever marry a man who molested a child, but it wasn't until after his death in 2016 that I learned Joanne had no idea. I should have known that, but in my naiveté, I assumed she knew the truth. He lied. My father told her that he met Anna at a grocery store when she was about twenty-one. He said the marriage broke up because she was far too young. He was very lonely when they met, and he thought she'd "grow up" more quickly than she had. He continued, summing up his marriage as "a mistake."

Following the couple's divorce, Simon and Joanne had a heated argument, and when he brought up Anna, she revealed what she was told. When Simon told her the truth, she shouted at him, saying he was lying. He then confirmed that she was "our sister," living with us for years, and that he had learned the truth from Anna. She wasn't even thirteen when Arthur started a sexual relationship with her. Joanne nearly passed out.

Chapter 31

Mia & Arthur & Joanne & Anita

I was always in love with California, having visited there for six consecutive summers. My original goal to move to California by 1980 was reached a few years earlier because I took a night job selling magazines on the phone, along with my day job, and saved enough money to move there in 1977.

I lived with my father and Joanne for a few months and then with Simon for two months until I could afford my own apartment. I rented a tiny one bedroom in Manhattan Beach. The novelty that never grew old in Miami Beach was going to the beach, and now I could do just that on the West Coast.

While living with my father and Joanne, my love for plants extended to their really ugly, little terrace—an overgrown jungle of so many dying plants and vines. It was one dreadful mess. I spent two full days fertilizing, potting, pruning, and transplanting the two dozen or so plants and made their terrace unrecognizably beautiful. It was done with so much love and care. I fondly remembered that day, as it was one of so few days that I felt the old man (the nickname we initially called our dad endearingly because age was never a sore spot for him) and his wife appreciated me and celebrated me for the good work I did on their behalf. It was pathetic. It was just a terrace. But their gratitude was so welcome and rare.

My tiny dwelling in Manhattan Beach was so wonderful, primarily because it was a few blocks from the beach. I loved decorating my apartment, and I couldn't wait to have girlfriends and boyfriends over.

One night after living there for a few weeks, I saw Roy Firestone, a guy I knew of from Miami Beach High, on KCBS, one of the network affiliates in Los Angeles. He was the station's sports anchor. I didn't know him personally in high school, but everyone knew who he was. I called him at the station.

"Hi, Roy. We both went to Beach High, and I just moved out here a few months ago. I'm finally living in my own apartment in Manhattan Beach, and I have almost no friends yet. I was very excited to see you on TV and wanted to know if we could get together."

"I don't know, Mia. People call me all the time under false pretenses. Can you just maybe tell me who some of your friends were at Beach High? It'll make me more comfortable, since we didn't really know each other. If that's okay, before I commit to getting together?" he asked. He was always very polite.

I started throwing out names of friends. I mentioned my BFF Wendy, and they knew each other. I mentioned a few others he knew as well. Finally, he agreed to meet me for dinner on a Saturday night a few days later.

When he picked me up, he was so warm and kind. We started dating. He was thoughtful and attractive and treated me so well. I was never really sure why it didn't work out, but after about eight months, we went our separate ways. Yet, it was always pleasant when we randomly ran into each other over the years.

I saw Roy again at Beach High's tenth reunion in 1981, the only one I went to because of the mostly sad memories of living there. We had fun that night, and that's where I bought the amazing photo book *Miami Beach*, by Gary Monroe and Andy Sweet, two Beach High alumni. Years later, Roy hosted his own sports program on ESPN that was incredibly successful, and he was happy to interview my public relations clients whenever I could provide a sports angle. His interviews were legendary. And my clients loved him and loved the interviews he did for them.

Roy didn't know it, but for years, he caused a lot of trouble between me and my first husband. It seemed to my then-husband Rob that every time we were in Miami Beach to visit my mother, Roy's program would be on television in every bar or restaurant we frequented. He was that popular. And Rob was that jealous. It was crazy.

In 1996, when we moved to Bel Air and Michael joined the Little League in Sherman Oaks, Roy was there with his sons. He also was a keynote speaker in the Little League. He was a celebrity. And at the park, I pretended I didn't see him when he walked right by me. It was truly an Academy Award winning act, the masterful way I ignored him. It was immediately followed by my husband, huffing and puffing, "There goes your boyfriend." Rob hated the sight of him. He couldn't handle being around him—even on television. He made it very difficult for me. He was so jealous that Roy dated me before I dated him, and he was also extremely jealous of Roy's success, even though Rob himself was successful. It was all so unpleasant and unnecessary. And I was so sad that Rob seemed so angry and controlling.

In 2009, only a year before we separated, my son and I had lunch with Roy to ask Roy if he could help Michael find a broadcasting job in sports. I was a nervous wreck. So worried and afraid that Rob would have a fit when we got home—even though I had told him that the three of us were lunching together—that I made a complete ass of myself at lunch. I got tongue-tied, tried to pressure Roy into finding a job for Michael, talked very fast and very loudly, and just generally embarrassed myself.

We didn't speak again for nearly eleven years, when I called him from Sacramento in 2020. Michael was pursuing a specific sports broadcasting job and needed a stellar reference. Roy couldn't have been nicer or more accommodating. It was then that I told him for the first time how he was the source of so much angst with my husband. He was truly stunned. We're still friends today, and he has written several fantastic letters to sports media on Michael's behalf.

∾

My cat and I lived in the tiny Manhattan Beach apartment until 1980, nearly three years. While I was so careful not to repeat my promiscuity from college, in which I still felt ashamed, I did date but with more discretion. I still wanted to get married and have children, hopefully before I turned thirty.

Rob and I married two-and-a-half months before my thirtieth birthday, on September 11, 1983. It became a tough date to have as an anniversary. And on our nineteenth anniversary, we were featured on CNN for a three-minute story. In 2002, as a media relations consultant for the University of Southern California hospitals, one of my CNN contacts asked me if I had any compelling 9/11 stories with doctors, nurses, or other staff at the hospitals I represented. I mentioned my wedding date in passing, along with a couple of other ideas, never thinking my anniversary date would interest her. That evening the reporter contacted me and wanted to pursue my story, made more appealing by the fact that every year we went to Malibu, to the site where we were married to celebrate the day. The reporter and crew met us at Pepperdine University's chapel and taped the interview. Before the interview was over, the producer reminded us that our microphones were hot, and they could hear us arguing in the back of the church between shooting.

While I was living in Manhattan Beach, Simon graduated the University of California, Berkeley, in 1981. I was so very proud and excited for my little brother. We talked at least twice a month about what was going on in our lives. Our love lives. Simon's school life. My work life. We would compare notes on the old man and Joanne. And we speculated about Anna, but neither of us would be ready to contact her for years. For me, it was because my mother and father had indoctrinated us to see Anna as "the vixen," a scheming young girl who stole my father from my innocent mother. We were so thoroughly brainwashed that I couldn't imagine betraying my parents by seeing "my sister" who was "evil," even though I always adored her and had wanted to see her for years.

Mia McDaniel

The big day was coming and I planned to make the six-hour drive to see Simon graduate. I was thinking about who I would ask to take the drive with me when Simon called. He told me that our father was doing everything he could to prevent me from attending. He went further, telling my brother that he actually forbid my attendance. Not only would he not attend, he ranted, but said he would take Simon out of his will and might not speak to him for years. The reason he didn't want me to be there is a mystery. What Simon and I supposed was plain and simple—he just didn't want me there. He wanted to celebrate his son's graduation without the distraction of his oldest child, a daughter, who he didn't care about nearly as much. "I think it was just his way of keeping your war going. Keeping you away from me, knowing full well that that would hurt you. There's really no good explanation," Simon said.

That was it. I couldn't go and I was heartbroken. Once again, I wasn't present at an event for Simon, this one being the biggest of his life thus far. And as it turned out, our dad left nothing to Simon or me in his will.

My mother flew in for the ceremony. She wasn't going to miss her son's graduation. Even after what my father did to her and then prohibiting me from attending. One could argue that she did so because she was a loving mother. But it was much more complicated than that. She still enjoyed the sick flirtation she and her ex-husband shared every time they got together. And my father still loved it too. It was pathetic. I wouldn't see my little brother until weeks later when he drove down to Manhattan Beach, and we celebrated his graduation with Anita at an expensive Manhattan Beach restaurant that we hardly ever frequented because we couldn't afford it. The waitress came by to take our drink orders. She started to ask what we would like, when she noticed a plastic bag on the floor near Simon's foot. She picked it up, showed it to Simon and asked if it was his. "No, thank you......YES, YES, IT IS." She handed him the bag with three Thai sticks (originating in Thailand, a Thai stick is cannabis in leaf form, twisted into a small, tightly packed cylinder ready for smoking) that we took to my house and smoked after dinner.

~

I was thrilled to live in Manhattan Beach. Walking distance from the ocean. Just two and a half blocks away. Near Moon's Market where everyone in the area shopped. It was truly astounding years later when Rob and I were selling our second house and a family came to see it. The Chinese American father/husband asked me if I had lived in Manhattan Beach and frequented Moon's Market. When I said I had, he said, "I knew it. I'm Moon!"

Anita and I became roommates around the end of 1978, when we were both living in Manhattan Beach in very tiny apartments. We wanted to find a more spacious, two-bedroom apartment together. We found a wonderful place just a few blocks east of my first apartment and rented it. I stayed until I moved in with Rob in late 1980.

I made some incredible friends in Manhattan Beach and at the ad agency, including of course, my soulmate Michael. Anita remains my dearest, bestest friend today. If not for the Covid-19 pandemic, Anita would have joined me in California in the summer of 2020, for our third annual summer girls' week. The conference was canceled, and at that time, it was thought to be too dangerous for Anita to fly from Oklahoma City to join me.

~

Shortly before Anita and I moved in together, I was date-raped. I felt guilty about the rape for a long while, but it ran much deeper than simply the blame and the shame I felt for going out with a man who would ultimately rape me. It happens far too often, as was well documented by the Me Too movement. But for me, it opened my eyes a little more to the incredibly low self-esteem I had. The man who raped me should never have been someone whose invitation for dinner I accepted.

Mia McDaniel

He was a waiter at an upscale restaurant that Michael and I frequented for lunch downtown. He wasn't particularly smart or witty or anything I should have found desirable. The only thing that attracted me to him was his good looks. I knew I shouldn't have dinner with him. This was how badly I felt about myself. I told him to let me know where and I would meet him there. Good sense on my part, that I immediately lost when he told me he was preparing our dinner at his apartment. It would have been the perfect moment to cancel. But no, I followed him to his apartment near downtown Los Angeles. It wasn't a very nice building, nor was it in a very nice part of downtown.

Nevertheless, I met him in the garage, and we took the elevator to his unit. It was drab, ugly, and depressing.

He had set the table and prepared dinner for us, though I have no recollection of what he cooked. We drank some wine and moved to the couch. We started kissing, and it wasn't until then that my alarm bells finally sounded. What the hell was I doing with this man in this dreadful apartment? I finally had the sense to leave. But he wouldn't let me. At first he was sweet and acting romantically, teasing me, "You're so pretty. I'm so happy to be with you. Please don't stop me," he said.

"I'm so sorry, but I have to go home. I didn't feed my cat this morning, and I need to buy cat food, too," I said, naively, thinking he would actually let me go. He didn't and he became more aggressive. I still expected him to stop and said once more, "C'mon, you said you loved cats. My poor guy is so hungry. We can get together another time," knowing full well that would never happen. He continued his despicable behavior, pulling at my blouse and my jeans.

When he said, "I'm a man and men have certain needs," I knew I'd lost the battle and it would be in my best interest to submit and carefully excuse myself to get home safely. When it was finally over, I very sweetly and calmly thanked him for dinner and left as fast as I could.

It was a seminal moment for me. As I drove home crying, I realized that I was lucky to have escaped and that I would try so hard to stop making the same bad decisions I made for so many years. To care for myself more and not date any man who was truly not worthy of my time, let alone anything more.

I shared the experience with Michael, who visited the waiter at his restaurant and verbally accosted and scared the fuck out of him. Michael then assured me that it was highly unlikely the rapist would ever rape anyone again. I also shared my anguish with Anita, who told me over and over again that I was wonderful and that I needed to believe in myself more. And that it happened to her, too, before we were friends and she had also tried to assert better judgment since her rape.

∾

Anita was always privy to my father's behavior. There were many Sunday afternoons or evenings when I just wanted to call him, and she would urge me not to. We spoke about this recently and recalled an evening when we were having dinner at the former Moustache Café in Westwood. Upon walking into the small alcove before being seated, I had another moment where I wanted to speak with my father. Neither of us remembered why I did, but we remembered the consequences of me not listening to my dear friend and calling him from the pay phone in the restaurant. We left before dinner because I was sobbing. He just didn't want to talk to me and, once again, I couldn't handle it. And once again, Anita tried to so hard to prevent me from myself.

Anita understood me the way best friends do. She saw everything that my father did to me and how hard I tried to make my relationship with him better. She saw how when I was disappointed or saddened or experiencing a real loss, that it took me so long to recover.

"She holds on to anything bad that happens to her, and it takes so long for her to let it go. I've been there. I've seen it. It made me so sad. She had guilt over her mother's death for years, even though she did everything a daughter could possibly do and more for her mother. It's another consequence of having little security, kindness, or attention paid to her by her mother and father," she told Anna years later.

On January 30, 1980, my beloved oma died. She had had a massive stroke two years before and succumbed to the illness. I was devastated. And it was Anita's birthday.

There was no email. There was no way to print out an airline ticket. You had to go to the ticket counter at the airport or hire a travel agent. Anita was a godsend. She drove to LAX, used her credit card, and bought a round-trip ticket home for me to leave for Miami Beach the next day. And she helped me pack and drove me to the airport in the morning. She's always been that supportive. For forty-four years, so far.

Chapter 32
Rob & Mia

I met my first husband, Rob Liano, when we both worked at a major advertising agency in Los Angeles. He had been recently transferred from the New York headquarters. We shared a few clients and loved talking about New York. We got to know each other and it was exciting. We started dating. He came to Manhattan Beach on the weekends, and I often spent the night at his apartment in Los Feliz, which was much closer to our office than my apartment.

He had a truly wonderful extended Italian family. Rob's mother was one of ten children. His grandparents, his mother, and his uncle Willie and aunt Jo lived in a beautiful home in a New Jersey suburb, about forty-five minutes from the city. I met all the uncles and aunts and cousins, and it was so warm, so comforting, and so much family. It was completely different from my family in the best way. To this day, I have a relationship with Aunt Jo, one of the few relatives still alive. Rob would be livid if he knew, as he prohibited me from talking to the family when we divorced in 2011. When I tried, he found out and forced his mother to write me a letter explaining that she could not speak to me because her son was too angry and didn't want us to be in touch. And when I sent Nana a birthday present, he insisted she send it back to me. I knew all this because Nana told me. Even though we were divorced, it made me so sad and brought back unhappy memories of my father trying to control my actions.

Nevertheless, I'm excited that I'm still in contact with Aunt Jo and sent her some love for her one hundredth birthday in 2022,

Mia McDaniel

and Uncle Sammy, whom I always adored, turned one hundred in 2018, and I was thrilled to be in touch with him. And Uncle Dom at ninety-six, whom I called my "Jewish uncle" because sometimes Jews and Italians are so much alike. I dearly miss not being in touch with most of the family and was heartbroken when Nana died in 2018, and Rob didn't want me to attend the funeral.

Rob is an intellect. My father was an intellect. They both prided themselves on intellectual endeavors. For Rob it was the *New York Times* crossword puzzle on Sundays. He claimed the puzzles on the other days were "too easy." He read the biographies of Benjamin Franklin and Thomas Jefferson. Of Spalding Gray and Sam Shephard. He did not watch television except for New York Yankee baseball games and an occasional PBS program. Though he did love *The Sopranos*, one of the very few shows we ever watched together. My father's intellectual endeavors leaned toward the scientific. He devoured everything written by or about Albert Einstein and Stephen Hawking. He graduated college as a physicist.

Rob also prided himself on a complete lack of knowledge or interest in popular culture. If it was in *People* magazine or on the entertainment page of *USA Today*, he wanted no part of it. And *Entertainment Tonight* was especially distasteful. At first, his philosophy was sexy. I always liked intelligent men. He was attractive and treated me well. And we shared stories. Of our families. Our New York upbringing. And our goals.

Eventually, Rob became a bore and a source of problems. He was a different kind of narcissist than Arthur. He was more of an academic narcissist, whereas my father had a God complex. They both had volatile tempers (as Italians and Jews frequently do) and believed that they were smarter than most people. Rob, however, could be kind and was always ready to defend me when my father and Joanne were often cruel to me. The two men got along rather well. Arthur was impressed by his son-in-law. So impressed that he embarrassed and hurt me when he asked me, "Do you swing from chandeliers for Rob? You're so lucky to have him. I can't imagine what you must do in the bedroom for him." I was crushed. I abhorred the sexual reference and was so sad that my father didn't think Rob was lucky to have me as his wife. I foolishly sought solace from my mother, who found it rather funny, and said, "Oh, so what. It's pretty funny. He's your father, let it go."

Rob wrote in a journal. He likely had three or four dozen journals during our marriage. They were birthday presents. Chanukah presents. Christmas presents. Father's Day presents from me and the kids. As soon as he finished the one he was writing in, we would buy him another one. This was sexy too. At first.

He took up poetry, seriously after writing "So Six" when Samantha was six. We were in our second house, this one in Burbank, where Michael was born. Both children were born at Cedars-Sinai (I was thrilled to see the Jewish star at the top of the hospital by the name contrasting where we got married with the cross on top of the chapel), which was quite the schlep from the eastside and Burbank.

Rob hated his job. "Advertising is not a cure for cancer. It's a group of young and middle-aged men and some women talking about cat food. And beer." He stayed because there was talk of the agency going public. In a few years at most. Maybe. Probably. He was far more interested in writing poetry than running the agency's media department. But he always worked very hard to support his growing family. He worked late. He traveled. He was very conscientious. He was promoted multiple times at multiple large, international agencies in his career. When he finally retired, he was senior vice president/media director.

He was an excellent father until we divorced in 2011 when the kids were grown. There was no doubt that he adored his children. He went to all of Michael's baseball games when he played second base in junior high and high school at Campbell Hall, though Rob did a fair share of bitching. Rob and Michael watched baseball games together and traveled to numerous ballparks across the country,

Mia McDaniel

the most special being Yankee Stadium to see the games in person. And he helped Sam read lines when she wanted to be an actress. He recounted how he was "a starving actor" himself in both New York and Los Angeles, the first time he moved there years before we met.

But like my father, he was selfish. He had to go to the office; he didn't want to go to the office. He wanted to write poetry. And he didn't have the patience to treat me like a lady. I desperately wanted my husband to open the car door for me, to help me with my coat, to say, "After you" and hold the door when entering a restaurant. I asked him repeatedly to please do that for me. He would do it once or twice after I asked and then he would tell me he didn't really want to do that. It just wasn't important to him, and it really hurt me.

He especially didn't want anything to do with the mundane maintenance or repairs for any of the four homes we owned over time. I was responsible for everything about the house. The plumbing, the electrical, the appliances. If there was mold. Or if the air conditioning wasn't working. One time in Encino, where we lived in our fourth home, I pointed out a small, brown spot and what looked like a leak in the living room ceiling. He couldn't be bothered and said, "Mia, just deal with it. Call someone to look at it. I can't be bothered with this never-ending house crap." That was his attitude for small jobs (light bulbs, A/C filters) and big jobs (painting the house, getting a new dishwasher when the old one broke). He would have let the ceiling rot. I called a roofer. He told me that for the previous homeowner, the cable company had installed the antenna by nailing it into the roof. The cable company had caused the leak, and they needed to repair it. Even then, Rob refused to help. I got the cable company to repair it and pay us damages. When my father and I were on good terms, he was always willing to repair minor problems in two of our four homes. It was a great help.

We rarely communicated when we bought our first house because my father had discarded me five years earlier. Just like he discarded Anna. I remember what he said to me so vividly, but

I cannot remember why he said it. It was 1978, and I was working as a reporter for an advertising trade magazine, and we were on the phone. He got very angry and said, "Mia, I want you to pretend that I'm dead," and he hung up on me. I started to cry and one of my fellow reporters was so kind and said I should leave the office (it was likely an hour or less before quitting time) and he walked me to my car.

For our second and third homes, however, it was a little easier because we could count on him to fix little things like replacing the garbage disposal or repairing a wobbly shelf. Rob would help him, and I always felt special when they would work on the house. My father and I called Rob "Arthur's apprentice." I was so grateful for those times; one would have thought the two men built me a new wing, instead of simply repairing small items.

In the last few years of our Mulholland home and then in Encino, my father was unavailable again because he decided we weren't speaking, and eventually, because of his deteriorating health. Not having my father repair things for us was challenging, but it was about far more than a leaky faucet. We could afford a repairman. There was something wonderful about him coming to my house and fixing something that was broken. It meant the world to me and was always a good reason to ask him to visit. He liked the role, and we couldn't thank him enough. We were delighted that he was so good at helping us, especially since we didn't have a clue and he was so handy and smart. We praised him ad nauseam.

The constant upkeep of living in each house was proving very difficult for me to handle alone. And I was also working as a freelance publicist out of our homes since 1987, two years after our daughter was born. I had worked at numerous large public relations firms until 1985 when I got pregnant. I was summarily fired for being pregnant. I filed with the Equal Employment Opportunities Commission (EEOC), and after a few years, I won the case. It was such vindication. And years later when I mentioned it to a client, she exclaimed, "That was you? I know about you! I had worked for the same agency before this position. So many people know about you and admired what you did!"

I was so thrilled to hear that. But while I won the case, I was out of a job. I knew someone who knew someone who hired me as a freelancer, and I worked for her agency for many years. Within a couple of years, I branched out and freelanced for the biggest PR firms in Southern California and New York from our breakfast nook until we could afford a house with an office, which wasn't until December 1992. This was in the early eighties. There weren't that many women working from home.

I remember talking to a reporter at the *Los Angeles Times* and asking him to hold for a minute (I was watching Michael take his first step). He rudely said, "Why? Are you a working mother who needs to check on her kids?" And then, he hung up. I called him back and asked if it was something I said. He laughed and apologized, and we worked together again. But the media did not appreciate mothers working from home. Neither did clients. For years.

In 1989, when I started working with my now second husband, he made certain that if a client or a media representative (writer, reporter, producer, on-air talent) wanted to speak with me, they would take a message and let me know and I called them back. This way "the horror" of working from home wasn't divulged. There was no "caller ID." They thought I worked at his office. My business cards had his office number first and then my home phone number, as if it was a second location for the firm.

Chapter 33
Ryan

My stepbrother, Ryan, was born in March of 1980. I heard about his birth from Aunt Jean. She hadn't given it much thought when in her excitement, she called me celebrating the birth of Arthur's second son. She was elated. I thanked her for calling, hung up, and sobbed. And then I realized that I was happy the baby was a boy. I would be his only daughter. For the rest of his life.

We met in 1986 when he was six. Ryan and my father joined us for a barbeque in our first home. It was a pleasant meeting, and it went well, but he didn't visit us again until we were in our Mulholland home in 1996. During that time, we were together a few times at my father and Joanne's home, but there were always plenty of people there, and we had little time alone. Over the years I called him, but whenever I reached him, he said he was very busy but would be happy to call me back. He never did.

I'm certain the reason we never bonded was because Joanne poisoned the well when he was a little boy and continued to brainwash him until she was unable to manipulate him anymore. It made me sad to think I had a little brother whom I rarely saw. Although at my father's apartment when he and Joanne were divorced, I was visually assaulted by so many framed photographs of Ryan (and Simon) and none of me.

It was a startling and welcome surprise when at my father's funeral in 2016 Ryan came over to me as soon as I walked into the room and hugged me. I felt so sad that a simple hug meant so much to me and immediately went to "my guilty place" that it was my fault we hadn't been closer. I thought about it for days, and finally realized it wasn't me. It was Joanne. She didn't want him to have anything to do with me, her husband's other child. I was unwanted competition. She made that point stunningly clear when she convinced my father to name their business The Ryan Simon Company, for his two sons.

Chapter 34

Mia & Rob & Arthur & Rose & Sam & Michael

I wanted to share my life with my parents so badly. I was heartbroken that they weren't there when I was growing up.

My father did not walk me down the aisle when I married Rob, though he was alive and well and lived nearby, but Simon did. (We did not invite my father to our wedding because he had been treating me so horribly.) He did not come and see me when I sent him a card to tell him that I was pregnant with his first grandchild. And when I called him as well, he responded with, "What do you want, Mia? Do you expect me to throw you a party?" He did not visit me at Cedars-Sinai when Sam was born. And, when he had the opportunity to be there when Michael was born, he declined.

They weren't there for me when I had children. When Sam was born, we were beyond ecstatic. We wanted a girl, and she was perfect. Our hearts grew bigger, and we couldn't imagine how we ever lived without her. And Rob agreed to name our little girl Samantha, for my beloved oma. We called her Sam. Sam was born on October 24, and I never forgot that that was one day before Anna's birthday on October 25. After all those years.

My mother and Nana both came to Los Angeles around my due date. Nana was staying three weeks; my mother one. She had to work. Nana was retired (They told us not to hire any help because they would be with us.) When Sam was three days old, Nana's father, Rob's "Grandpa," had a cerebral hemorrhage, and at ninety-two, the doctors thought he would die. Nana took the next plane back home. He survived. Thank God we still had my mother. We thought and hoped that she would stay longer since we purposely had not arranged for help. And it was a difficult delivery, twenty-two hours in labor and an emergency Caesarean section. My mother looked at me as if I had two heads, "I can't stay any longer. I have my business (she had started a small clothing boutique at the nail salon she frequented). And my cats (eight of them) who need me too. (She had hired someone to look after them while she was gone.)" We were floored and disappointed. Again. Rob had to work in a few days. It's not like we needed or wanted a full-time au pair, but we did need some warm and fuzzy family help. My father wasn't in the picture, and it's unlikely we would have asked him anyway. He was useless when it wasn't about him. We managed. Of course. We always did without my parents by our side. My BFF Michael was an enormous help, even though he had already been diagnosed with ARC (Aids Related Complex—the precursor to AIDS in the early days). He visited once a week, bringing lunch with him from Cantor's Deli on Fairfax, and he helped me with the laundry.

My labor with Michael had started in the early afternoon of October 6, 1988, and Rob rushed me to the hospital (Sam was in preschool, and Rob had arranged for a neighbor to pick her up and stay with her). By coincidence, my father and Joanne were surprising us by stopping by to say hello. They had only done that once before, so I foolishly thought they were being especially kind and wanted to see if we needed anything, as our baby was due that day.

As it turned out, we did need help. Rob's mother (Nana) was arriving in a few hours from New Jersey. There would be no one to pick her up at the airport because Michael was going to be born. While I was lying in the backseat crying, I saw my dad peek in and look at me, with what I idiotically thought was genuine concern. Rob asked his father-in-law if he could please help us out and pick Nana up at the airport. We had never asked him to do anything for us before, other than playing "handyman" at our house, tasks he was so happy and proud to carry out. There were no cell phones. Rob couldn't contact his mother. And Arthur was about to be a grandfather for the second time and hadn't been present the first time. I heard my father say something about an eye doctor's appointment he couldn't miss. But I wasn't really paying much attention.

Not only did my father and Joanne refuse to pick Nana up, but they also told Rob they wouldn't be at the hospital either. "Rob, it's very difficult to get an appointment with this eye doctor. It took me five weeks. I have to go see him," my father said, defending his position. He wished us good luck and sped off. Good luck? What an asshole. Rob reached the airline eventually, and they paged Nana. It took almost two hours before she heard the page. She got a cab and took it directly to Cedars.

Who ignores their pregnant daughter, in labor and about to give birth, for an eye doctor? He wasn't going blind. It was a routine appointment, and he just couldn't be bothered with rescheduling. He needed "a better reason" than his daughter giving birth. Michael was born by emergency Cesarean section a few hours later, and we fell deeply in love with our little son and couldn't believe he wasn't always in our lives.

Chapter 35
Mia & Rob & Arthur & Joanne

It was in 1988 when Rob and I clearly became "the glue holding the family together." It started in 1986 when Sam was almost a year old and Simon had arranged for my father and me to get together after several years, and continued until my father had no more use for me.

With rare exceptions, every birthday, holiday, anniversary, or other celebration was arranged by us and held at our house until we divorced. Because I still desperately wanted my father's love and approval, the guests would always include him and Joanne, (when we were speaking) along with Simon and his wife Danielle, and later Simon and his wife, Sophia, and my mother and any other family if they were in town. And, when it was a big celebration, friends of ours were also there.

Holding the family together was quite a departure from earlier times, following his "I want you to pretend I'm dead" statement. I was unable and unwilling to do that, but we didn't speak for years. I'm convinced that Joanne must have persuaded him that he didn't need me in his life anymore. She was fine with Simon but not with Arthur's first born.

After he said that, I was astonished. Confused. I called him repeatedly over the next few years, but he wouldn't take my call. The only time he did was when I disguised my voice and used a phony name when Joanne answered the phone. She put my dad on the phone. It was two days after my beloved oma died, and I just couldn't let that stand. Not because he didn't call me to express his sympathy—I in no way expected that—but because he hadn't called Simon. I was livid. Simon called me later that evening to tell me that our father had just called him to express his sympathies.

I have a lot of internal conflict about the emotional abuse and neglect I experienced as a child. But I wasn't physically beaten. I didn't go hungry. I was well-clothed. There are children who have a parent in jail. Children who are beaten. Hungry children. Children with few clothes who live in shelters or their mother's car. Still, I was distressed and troubled and had made a mess of some parts of my life because my father abused my cousin, cheated on my mother with said cousin in the same house as the three of us, and virtually ignored me because he wanted to and, hey, I wasn't a son. And later on, because his third wife expected him to do so?

After all, our family once lived in a five-bedroom "mansion" with a half-acre of forest behind us. My parents drove new cars. I had pretty clothes. Simon always looked so adorable and handsome. Nevertheless, when I didn't see a dentist; was forced to get undressed with unsolicited help from a male physician and no parent around; was constantly belittled by my father and told by my mother it didn't matter, it was still abuse. And there was neglect. Yet, I still tried to buy them. I bought them each a brand-new car. They always wanted and asked for more. They questioned everything I did. And if they didn't come first, they let me know they were "mortally wounded" to have me for a daughter.

So much of my turmoil was because when my father and I got along, I thought he was as crazy about me as I was about him. Yet I always knew he would find a reason to "break up with me" again and he wasn't as crazy about me as I hoped. Or as he pretended to be.

If not for a handful of good therapists (my father thought all shrinks were thieves) and my oma, I likely wouldn't be happily married today and share a warm, loving relationship with both of my children. Nevertheless, I carry the deep shame of my father's legacy with me.

Chapter 36

Rose & Mia & Rob & Simon

In 1988, Simon, Rob, my father, and I convinced my mother to move out west. She had recently packed up her apartment in Miami Beach and was planning to move to Kissimmee, Florida, and marry her latest boyfriend, a man she thought she loved, who was going to be her third husband. She changed her mind. She didn't really love him and she really didn't want to live in Kissimmee. Simon and I persuaded her to move to Southern California, where she had two children and two grandchildren. And she was already packed.

Rob and I found an apartment for her in the same apartment complex we first lived in as a couple and loved. My mother hated it. After living there a few weeks, an earthquake damaged all her good china and crystal. After a few months, the apartment was burglarized and all her jewelry (mostly costume) was stolen. She hadn't purchased renters' insurance, even though we told her it was essential. Her response was that she had never needed it in Florida. Clearly, those two incidents didn't help our argument that Southern California was preferable to Miami Beach. But she did have her entire family living close by. I thought our presence would trump everything. It was nonsense; believing that was absurd.

We all tried to so hard to make her comfortable and enjoy living in Southern California. Once again, I knew my mother expected me to put her first. It was always about her. Or my father. I suspect that within a few months of living in Los Angeles, she made up her mind that it wasn't going to work out. And, oh yeah, Arthur also convinced her that if Rob and I had found an apartment in a better location, in the San Fernando Valley, she would have been happier. He lived in Northridge. Of course, when my mother told everyone she would be moving to Southern California, Arthur didn't offer any help. Not at all. But he was so quick to criticize me whenever he wanted to embarrass or shame me. And I obsessed and worried for a long time that because of the apartment we picked for my mother, it was my fault that she wasn't happier, an unfortunate burden I shouldn't have ever had to carry.

My mother got a job at a jewelry store in her neighborhood. Not an especially luxurious one, but it "wasn't dreadful" was the best way I could put it. My mother made friends with Gene, the owner. And as she so often did, she believed people in authority more than her family. After all, he owned a jewelry store (which was impressive to no one besides her). Simon and I thought he was creepy. He claimed to know more about Southern California restaurants, entertainment, and shopping than anyone else. And he knew more about physicians and hospitals. My mother believed he could provide insight into anything she was interested in finding out about Southern California. Didn't matter to her that she had her entire family there. Who would care more about her and what she needed? Or wanted? Her family or Gene, the jewelry store owner? She chose Gene.

Within a few months, my mother needed to have a hernia repaired. I had been seeing a wonderful physician in Beverly Hills, who had delivered Sam and was my current obstetrician as I was very pregnant with Michael. I called her, and she recommended a specialist for my mother's hernia. My doctor and the one she recommended were affiliated with Cedars-Sinai, arguably the premier hospital in Southern California. Gene also recommended a physician, unbeknownst to me. I told my mother I would be happy to take her to the doctor and be another set of ears. She was relieved that I would accompany her.

I picked my mother up and was surprised when she wouldn't tell me the address right away, but instead told me to go east on the Ventura Freeway. Heading east was not the direction to Cedars-Sinai or even to Beverly Hills, but if this doctor was referred by my obstetrician, the location was irrelevant. It was a bit odd though to be heading away from the Westside. Soon, I was getting off the freeway in quite an impoverished neighborhood on the Eastside. I was shocked. "My doctor referred you to this 'Clinica' (a large sign in front of the ugly building said it was "La Clinica") in east Los Angeles?" "No." she replied. "This was the doctor that Gene, my boss, recommended." I was stunned. And very pissed off and worried, but thought I'd better let it go until we left. We walked into the doctor's private office. There was an ashtray filled with cigarette butts. The office was a pit. I sat quietly and knew I would do everything I could to talk my mother out of this lunacy. And I was almost eight months pregnant and not at all pleased or in a good mood anymore. And wanted to read my mother the riot act.

We left La Clinica and had a heated argument about her doctor. My mother said, "I'll think about it." There was no additional thought. But rather, there was a surgery date and a hospital. And it was with the physician we saw at La Clinica at an old run-down hospital in East Los Angeles that doesn't exist today. I was terrified for my mother and not happy about having to visit her in the unpleasant building while eight months pregnant. But I visited my mother daily for three days. So did my father, which once again was the highlight of my mother's day, complete with the requisite flirtations.

When she finally came home from the hospital, it was a few days before my baby shower for Michael that my dearest girlfriends had planned. I walked into Janine's home, and it was lovingly decorated with baby shower balloons and signs and crepe paper streamers. There were about twenty of my closest friends there. It was wonderful, though not as hilarious as Sam's shower when I and three of my four pregnant girlfriends I'd met at Jane Fonda's maternity workout showed up wearing the same exact dress. There's a wonderful photo of five enormous mothers-to-be, with four in the same ugly pink, blue, and yellow flowered dress with a white collar. There were so few fashionable maternity clothes at the time and even fewer shops. The big moment came when my mother arrived at the shower. It was to be a surprise because it so often had to be about her. Even when it wasn't. (It was the same stunt for Rob's surprise fiftieth birthday party that I threw. She pretended to be wishing him a happy birthday from Miami Beach, when she was just thirty minutes away.) For the baby shower, my mother insisted on driving to Janine's by herself, even though she was in pain and three of my friends had offered to drive her. She would have been much more comfortable, but she wanted to be the center of attention and spent the entire shower lying on Janine's sofa moaning. But she was not going to miss her daughter's second shower. She hadn't flown out for Sam's baby shower or for my wedding shower when I married Rob. Her behavior was an embarrassment. Before my mother arrived, it was fun. Afterwards, she wouldn't stop complaining to anyone who would listen. And when she wasn't complaining about her suffering, she complained about how angry she was with one of my friends. She said that the gift she bought on her behalf while she was hospitalized "was nothing like what we had talked about. I was so disappointed."

We continued to try. My mother wanted to move to another building at the very least. She found her own apartment, two blocks from the first one. Either Arthur hadn't even tried to talk her into the Valley, or he failed to persuade her. It was a little roomier, had more windows, and was in a newer building. But it wasn't right. She wasn't any happier there. And pretty soon there was talk of her moving back to Florida.

Chapter 37

Mia & Rob & Arthur & Joanne

I loved and needed to have my father share my life. So I chose to "forget" all the times he hurt me or wasn't there for me. When he just wasn't available to me: when I was little, just to talk to, or to play with. Or to just make me feel like he cared. Years later, he would accuse me of not inviting him and Joanne over often enough and how that hurt them. I was devastated and, in my hurt and anger, gathered a couple of dozen photos of parties and dinners and birthdays we hosted over the years and dropped them off in his mailbox. He never apologized. Or acknowledged the photos. I felt very small for sending them.

When Rob and I wanted to go out in the evening alone for dinner and a movie, there was only one time that my mother agreed to babysit, and it was because my father said he would join her and they would watch Sam together. They came over and babysat and reminisced. I found the relationship the two shared disgusting but was grateful to at least have my mother babysit one time.

Almost three years later when I was enormously pregnant with Michael, we got theater tickets at the last minute to see *Phantom of the Opera* in Century City (as an advertising executive, Rob was often the recipient of free theater, theme park, and concert tickets). I called my mother who lived close by to ask her to babysit. She refused. She was packing to move back to Florida and just couldn't stop. Her moving day was still three weeks away. And she had a small two-bedroom apartment. Not the house in New Jersey.

The trip to the theater and back home was awful. We ended up dropping Sam at Anita's house, which was nowhere near our house or the theater. The round-trip was more than three hours. I was once again forced to confront the reality that neither my mother nor my father would help out with their grandchildren. It wasn't all that surprising, as she wasn't there for us as children either. Not only was I physically uncomfortable but so very sad.

A few days before my mother moved back to Miami Beach, she told me that she was disappointed and even shattered by my behavior. I hadn't a clue as to what she was talking about. I knew I wasn't perfect, and I knew that she and my father were my biggest critics. And there were times when my mother and I argued. I did know, though, that I wasn't the most tactful person, but I had tried so hard to keep her happy and living nearby. And now she was leaving. But first she felt compelled to tell me, "Mia, you know the primary reason I'm leaving Los Angeles is because you don't have enough love in your heart for me. You only care deeply for Rob and the children, and there is no room for me."

What? Are you kidding me? I didn't say that, but instead tried to hold back my tears. I could barely speak; I was so deeply hurt and worried. Was I actually responsible for my mother's move 3,000 miles back to Miami Beach because I didn't have enough love in my heart for her? Because I loved my husband and children and tried my best to always be there for them, while trying to be there for her too? A foreign concept to my parents.

I presumed that's where her phony distress originated, as she couldn't conceive of putting her children and husband first. But instead of letting it go, I owned it and wondered how I could have done that to her. What was wrong with me? I was very depressed and held this in my heart for ten years, until I first started therapy and my psychologist sorted it out for me, "Mia, it was more likely that your mother didn't have room in her heart for you." It was just another in a series of manipulations by my selfish, childish, narcissistic parents.

A few days later, my father was at my house on Mulholland, and my mother was there too. She hadn't left for Florida yet. I felt it was time to summon up the courage and confront him about his relationship with Anna, with my mother right there to chime in if she wanted to. We were standing near the stairs to the second story. I had just shown both my mother and father Anna's letter. I regret that. They didn't deserve my allegiance, and Anna certainly didn't deserve that small betrayal. But I showed them the letter for "the right reasons." I wanted them to see in black and white what she told me about her relationship with my father. And for them to see how much she missed me. And how much she wanted to get together with me, a feeling I too shared. I looked my father in the eye and asked him, "When did your relationship with Anna begin?"

He knew damn well what I meant. I had never seen my father turn so very pale, as he lied to my face, stammering, "I never touched her until your mother and I were divorced." Not the truth. Not even close. Before it even came out of his mouth, I knew I would accept whatever he would say, with all my heart. I refused to think otherwise. I had to believe him. And my mother didn't utter a word. If he did what Anna said he did... No, it was just not possible. I refused to reconnect with Anna for another twenty-eight years. Except for a brief phone message I left with her babysitter a few months after receiving her letter.

Chapter 38
Mia and Best Friend Michael

In 1989 when Michael passed away, it was six days before Thanksgiving. Rob and I knew it would be good for us and our little children (Sam was four; Michael, one) to host Thanksgiving dinner, as we always did.

My father arrived on time. He was always punctual and mocked you if you weren't. About ten other guests were there, and we were waiting for a few more. Michael's parents were coming, too, having flown in earlier in the week from Maryland. First, they were going to visit three of Michael's closest friends' homes to say hello for the holiday. Everybody knew they didn't have to wait for them, but they wanted to. Simon told me a few days later about his conversation with the old man who said to Simon, "I don't care that their son just died. It's extremely rude of them to be late for Thanksgiving." Simon was speechless. Especially since he was this man's son.

As luck (or lack thereof in this case) would have it, my mother was visiting us, having arrived from Miami Beach to Burbank (where we lived in our second home) just two days prior. I let my mother know I was waiting to be picked up to go spread Michael's ashes over the Pacific. I told my father as well, as he had also dropped by. My mother gave me an ugly look and said, "So I'm visiting from 3,000 miles away and you're going out? Do you really have to do this?" I had been crying my heart out for the past three days, could barely speak, and was now forced to "justify" why I had to leave my mother. For a few hours. And she was not alone. She was with Arthur and Rob and her four-year-old granddaughter and infant grandson.

The hurt kept piling on. I "never" did anything right as far as my parents were concerned. It was still "all about them" and always would be. And I once again looked inward and questioned myself. About leaving my mother with family for a few hours while I left to spread my best friend's ashes. They were still as selfish and narcissistic as when they first married thirty-seven years earlier.

Chapter 39
Mia & Rob & Sam & Michael

Rob and I spoiled our children. We did everything we could to give them a happier life than either of us had. We weren't harsh or even mild disciplinarians. But we did everything we could to keep them safe, healthy, and happy. Not to say they didn't have any problems. Of course they did. But Sam and Michael, now at thirty-six and thirty-three, respectively, are "kids" that I couldn't be prouder of. They are kind. They are caring. They are generous and thoughtful. And they understand. And they have pursued what they love.

Michael loved baseball from the time he was three when Rob arranged for us to be on the field at Dodger Stadium for a media day. He was on Campbell Hall's junior and senior varsity baseball teams, and when Michael was a senior, the team competed in the Regional Championships in their Southern California division. Rob, Sam, Uncle Simon, and I drove to a college baseball field in Riverside and watched the nail-biting final playoff game. My father and I weren't speaking at the time, and once again, I was so sad that he wouldn't be part of this enormous event for his grandson, though I suspected that Simon told him about it the next day.

They won. Michael has a stunning, huge ring that resembles a Super Bowl ring, and his name is on a giant banner with the rest of the team, proudly hanging in the school's gymnasium in perpetuity. I was so excited when my father came to Michael's baseball games. He came twice. Michael was on the two teams for four years.

And Sam. She loves to act. She was the star in of every play in high school, like when she played the princess in *The Princess and The Pea*. Unless she preferred a different role, like when she wanted to be the dentist in *Little Shop of Horrors*. And she was. She won trophies and awards for acting. She even got high praise from some of the celebrity parents. My father did not attend one of his granddaughter's plays. It just wasn't convenient, or it was at a bad time. Or he was just too tired. Or he wasn't speaking to me. Yet I was always thinking about him and what I could do to make him love me. At Sam's annual school auction, I purchased a signed script from an episode of *The West Wing*, my father's favorite television show at the time. He loved it, but he didn't understand how thrilled I was to have had successfully bid on that for him. He came to expect gifts from me.

Sam wanted to be on television and in the movies and commercials. She got her first commercial at six years old. Then, just when an audition went extremely well and the producer wanted to see her again for an upcoming sit-com, Sam was bored. She didn't want to pursue acting anymore. She loves to write and has written pilots and screenplays and a book.

I loved being a mother more than anything, but at times when I was exhausted from work or carpooling, I didn't always feel like seeing another rehearsal. Or another ballgame. Most of the time I adored watching them play baseball or perform in the school's plays. And I was determined not to ever parrot my parents' bad behavior in any way. One of the best compliments I ever received was when my brother Simon told me, "I am so jealous of Michael's childhood. He has the best life. I wish our parents would have treated us like you and Rob treat him."

My children's biggest complaint growing up was that I was far too protective of them, which comes as no surprise considering my own parents lack of protection.

∿

In 2003, we found a chihuahua while dining at a local restaurant. He got out of his backyard and was lost, so we took him home. Rob and Sam quickly penned a dozen signs and posted them where we found the little guy. It was close to midnight when the owner saw the sign, called us, and came over to our house and was thrilled that we found his beloved little "Chiquito." For me, it brought back memories of when I was a little girl in New Jersey and our boxer, Betty, would get out of the backyard, and my dad and I would drive through the neighborhood calling her name and looking for her. We always found her. It was one of very few sweet memories I had of my dad.

The following week we went to the pet store in West Hollywood, where Chiquito was adopted, and we adopted Mick, a rather small long-haired chihuahua. It was 2003. While the kids adored Mick, Michael always wanted a big dog. I couldn't forget Simon's terrible accident with a German shepherd, and I didn't want to chance it with my children. Mick was our beloved dog, until he fell ill and died at age seventeen in 2020.

Mia McDaniel

Chapter 40
Mia & Rob & Sam & Michael

It was December 1992, and we had lived in our Mulholland Drive home for a few days when Sam (seven) and Michael (four) and I were eating dinner in the breakfast nook off the kitchen that faced the front of the house and the west side. It was adjacent to the long, steep driveway of the neighbor directly above us. It was 6:00 p.m. Sam got up to go to the bathroom. I was annoyed because I was hoping to have one family dinner without one of the kids getting up, and Rob was due home any minute. Sam's chair was directly in front of the window that overlooked two trees, flowers, and a fence, next to the neighbor's driveway. Moments later, there was a gigantic crash, and we watched a tree on our side of the driveway crash into our breakfast nook window. Apparently, Patsy, the homeowner had neglected to set the emergency brake on her Ford Bronco, and it slid down the hill from her home and crashed into our tree. At the exact moment that I screamed, Rob pulled into the garage and ran up the front steps. It was complete chaos. Michael was crying. He had some cuts and bruises on his face. Sam, thank God, was just coming out of the bathroom and was fine. Her seat was the closest to the incoming tree. I was so grateful my little girl had gotten up from the dinner table.

The homeowners, whom we had not met yet, having lived in the house for only four days, sent their Spanish-speaking housekeeper to our house. We couldn't communicate with her, and evidently, Patsy was too afraid to come over and see the damage for herself. She called her husband, Neal, a top neurosurgeon at UCLA Ronald

Reagan Medical Center, and he was home in about fifteen minutes, a drive that was typically more than forty minutes at that time of day. He introduced himself and offered to do anything he could to make sure we were all okay and to have the damage repaired. I was extremely stressed and worried about Michael, and was especially grateful that our new neighbor was a physician and could do a perfunctory examination right away. He also agreed to help schedule a follow up with a colleague of his at UCLA.

"We'd really appreciate it if you could have a look at Michael and make sure he's all right. And, after that, can you please arrange for a doctor from UCLA to come over and see him?" Rob said. "This is really overwhelming and we are very upset and I hope you will do everything you can to make sure Michael is ok. This is not the way we wanted to meet our new neighbors."

"I agree and I am so, so sorry this happened," Neal said, (meanwhile I'm sure he's thinking, "My wife's an idiot"). "I'll look at Michael and then call a physician right away. We will do everything we can to make this right."

We sat on the living room sofa with Sam, all of us in shock at how surreal it all was, as Neal arranged for a physician to come by at ten the next morning, as he thought Michael was fine with just some small scrapes and bruises. "Looks like a few cuts and scrapes, nothing to worry about." Then, Neal called a window company to come board up the window, until it could be replaced. We didn't call my father for comfort or help, as we knew it would be a wasted effort. There was nothing in it for him.

The next morning, Neal's colleague came to the house and concurred with Neal that Michael was fine. He told me and Rob to please feel free to call if we had any questions or issues.

The insurance company took care of the damage. We had no desire to sue our new neighbors. We just wanted the damages repaired. For weeks, Neal checked on Michael. At one point, when I was horseplaying with Michael and lifted him up and over my

Mia McDaniel

shoulder too quickly, he started to cry. He said that his head hurt. I frantically called Neal's colleague. At first, the nurse practitioner refused to take my call. When I called back, his snobby secretary came on and said, "Who is this and what is this about? We don't know any Mia or Michael Liano." Furious, I responded, "Tell him it's Dr. Neal Watson's neighbor. The one that Neal's wife blew her Ford Bronco into their breakfast nook." Apologetic and a bit humbled, the doctor, with his very huffy British accent, immediately took the call. I explained what happened, and he was certain it was a result of the over-the-shoulder playing. If anything seemed off the next day, he would clear his calendar immediately to see Michael. When people poke fun at Los Angeles, I think it's for incidents like this one.

Years later, when my father suffered his first stroke, Neal reviewed all of his workups and wouldn't charge us. I made a spectacular gift basket (I later left the public relations world to form a gift basket business that wasn't very lucrative, before returning to public relations), and they were very appreciative. The Watsons moved two years later. Unfortunately, our relationship with them didn't develop and was never something we laughed about and said, "Remember how awful that was when your car ran into our tree and our breakfast nook, and now we're all good friends?"

I ran into Neal once more years later at the UCLA hospital when I was going to visit a friend. In fact, my friend was actually at the Santa Monica location, but I thought it was at the Westwood hospital where Neal practiced. While driving in the parking structure, I saw three helicopters and multiple police cars speeding toward the entrance. And there was press. Lots of press hurrying into the entrance beside me. I asked a guard what was going on, and he said, "Michael Jackson was just dropped off by ambulance in the emergency room. There's so much media here, I can't keep it secret." When they couldn't locate my friend and finally referred me to their Santa Monica location, I got in the elevator to leave the hospital and there was Neal. It had been a few years and a doctor of his stature was not accustomed to "a stranger" in the elevator saying hello to him. "Oh, hi Neal," I said. He glanced over at me as if to say, "What?" He didn't say it, but you could tell he was thinking, "I'm not Neal, I'm Dr. Watson." I said, "It's Mia, your former neighbor on Mulholland." He shook my hand, asked after the kids, and that was the last time we ever saw each other. I'd heard he and Patsy divorced shortly after they moved. I wondered if her stupidity had anything to do with it, as the Bronco incident wasn't the only time she demonstrated what a nitwit she truly was.

∾

On January 17, 1994, at 4:30 a.m., there was a 6.7 magnitude earthquake. The Northridge quake was one of the highest ever recorded in an urban area in North America. We lived in Bel Air, which was about forty-five minutes (on a traffic-free day) from the epicenter in Northridge, but it was directly across the Valley from us "as the crow flies." It was terrifying and by far the biggest quake our family ever experienced. For my father, too, who also lived in Southern California in 1971 during the Sylmar earthquake—a 6.5 on the Richter scale. Even though 6.5 and 6.7 seem relatively close mathematically, they are not when earthquakes are measured. Each increase of 0.2 is approximately a doubling of the energy released.

Rob and I ran upstairs and grabbed Sam and Michael. As previously instructed, we went under our biggest, strongest piece of furniture, the dining room table. While running to the table, we looked out of the enormous living room windows and saw all the lights in the San Fernando Valley dimming and going out. Sparks flying. Then it was pitch black. We heard car sirens blaring and a strange hissing sound. A huge water tower way above the street, but not directly over our house, was leaking. Water was rushing down our private road. (It was a small, dead-end street directly above Mulholland Drive, but sharing the name, Mulholland Drive.) I did my best to remain calm and keep the children safe, but I was terrified.

Mia McDaniel

Our house kept shaking and it would continue intermittently for weeks. The big kitchen window, next to the living room but separated by a wall, was completely blown out. There were broken picture frames, wine bottles, and various other glass items all over the carpet. And we were lucky.

The only serious damage we suffered was the chimney. And we didn't know that until the end of the year when we had it inspected before using it. Every year we purchased a half cord of wood for the wood-burning fireplace that we loved in the winter months. The chimney looked fine in the living room and above the home through the roof. But, when inspected, we were told it had to be torn down and replaced. It was damaged beyond repair. With Rob's history of not paying attention to household problems, I was so grateful that we had the sense to check our chimney before lighting a fire. And our earthquake insurance covered the rebuilding of the chimney, the mantle, the hearth, and replacing the window.

We couldn't stay in the house, not because of the repairs (though that would have been quite difficult) but because we had no water. And no power. And the aftershocks were dreadful. My cousin Rusty and his wife, Jane, invited us to spend a few nights at their house. Much to our chagrin, it turned out that in Santa Monica, where their house was, the aftershocks were far worse because of the soil composition in the beach community. After two nights and several calls to our insurance company, we were put up in the Beverly Hilton Hotel at no expense to us. We stayed there for two weeks. It was Michael's turn the prior weekend to bring the elementary school rabbit, Persephone, home. She would have been returned the day of the earthquake but instead spent two weeks with us at the hotel.

In the afternoon after the earthquake hit, my father came by to see if we needed help. He checked on Joanne first, even though they were living separately and planning to get divorced, because she lived in the couple's former home in Northridge—the earthquake's epicenter. She suffered extensive damage and had to renovate most of the house. Particularly, the kitchen, as all of her cabinets literally fell off the walls. Her dishes, glasses, and anything breakable in the entire house was destroyed.

When I saw my father arrive, I was thrilled. "Daddy's here" was all I could think about. We'll be safe. He'll protect us. He didn't really do much, but his presence meant the world to me. As usual. As always. It was one of those times when we were on good terms, and I was grateful for that. And, as before on rare occasions, it gave me hope he could be the father I wanted and needed. Of course, once again, his true colors would ultimately prevail.

$\sim$

I had one grandparent still alive when we lived on Mulholland. Arthur's father, Papa, who was ninety-four. Papa and I weren't close. The only times I remember being with him, other than as a little girl, was when he and his second wife made their annual trek to Miami Beach for two months. They rented a small apartment, and they would invite me and Simon over for lunch for giant bowls of fresh strawberries and sour cream. It was one of the few traditions that I grew to love. Mostly because it was an actual tradition.

It was 1995 and I got a call from Simon that "the old man" had just called him and told him that Papa died. It was old age. I felt so sad that I didn't have any living grandparents. It was sad. I also despaired the next day that my father had called Simon but hadn't taken the time to call me.

I called my mother and told her that Papa had died earlier that day. And how did she respond? With, "That son-of-a-bitch. You don't know how many times he came onto me when I was married to your father." Really? I was once again stunned when I probably shouldn't have been. This time I told her that that was one of the most distressing things I'd heard her say in a while. "That's how you respond when your daughter calls to tell you that her grandfather died?" I said I needed to go and hung up after she tried to laugh it off.

She called me back a few minutes later and said, "You're right, Mia. I'm sorry." Over and over again my mother either made it about herself or tried to make me feel bad. Or both.

While I gave it little thought, I wasn't shocked that my mother said my grandfather had been inappropriate with his daughter-in-law. I found it sickening, but not all that surprising. With Arthur as my father, it wasn't a stretch to imagine my grandfather behaving improperly as well.

When Aunt Jean died in 1999, I was heartbroken. Aunt Jean was like a second mother to me. When I moved out west in 1977, my aunt was always there for me whether it was a shoulder to cry on over my father, or to celebrate my impending marriage or the birth of my children. I was crazy about Aunt Jean and loved when the two of us lunched together. Aunt Jean had been a constant in my life since I was twelve when Simon and I started our annual trek to California either with or to see our father. I called my mother. I was weeping when I told her that Aunt Jean had died late the night before after undergoing hip surgery. I was truly heartbroken at the loss of my wonderful aunt. And my mother? She said, "Mia, I didn't know you loved her that much." Another sickening comment that was so uncalled for and so unwelcome, particularly at such a vulnerable moment. As always, I questioned myself. I spent days trying to figure out if I was a drama queen or really loved my aunt Jean. There was no question. I loved and adored my dear, sweet, kind Aunt Jean and my mother would not ruin that with one painful comment.

Sam and Michael started elementary school when we lived on Mulholland. They attended the local public school, when Sam was in third grade and Michael was in kindergarten. It was a wonderful school that was more like a private school because it was in an affluent neighborhood. When they graduated elementary and then middle school, we wanted them to attend schools that prepared them for the future. Schools that provided the best education possible. Unfortunately, we knew that the public high schools in our neighborhood were inadequate. Rob and I wanted to do the best we could for our children.

When we enrolled the kids in private high schools, we didn't think about whom the other students' parents were and initially, were intimidated by the schools' star power. I was particularly uneasy because growing up I never knew how to act in front of people who had so much more than me. Not just materially, but in terms of maturity and poise. I frequently felt I couldn't relate and feared people wouldn't like me, causing me to try too hard.

Many of Sam and Michael's friends' parents were famous actors, directors, producers, and very wealthy people. Yet we were able to instill in them that while it was great fun to hang out with people who lived in amazing, expensive homes with swimming pools and movie theaters and refrigerators filled with foods you couldn't even imagine, what mattered most was being loved and connected and having a support system of parents who adored you and would always be there for you, no matter what. They would love you forever. There were a few unpleasant discussions about how our house "didn't stand up" when compared to their friends' houses. In short order, though, they got over it. Sam and Michael understood what mattered. Most of the time.

Honestly, it was me who was more intimidated by the celebrities than Rob or either of the kids. For the more than thirty years I lived in Los Angeles, I was "a celebrity slut," by my own admission. And I was so very excited when I heard that one of our neighbors on Mulholland had been a star on a well-known sitcom years before, and we became close friends. When Michael was still in elementary school, the father of one of his best friends was starring in a drama that was currently on the air. I must admit, it was fun chatting with him on a bench at school one day when another parent came by and asked if it was really him. That guy from the TV show.

Oh, the parties on Mulholland. No matter who was there, I was most excited when my father showed up. I treated him like royalty. He was my young, handsome, gregarious, sweet father who "mingled well" with all our friends. He seemed to enjoy spending time with me and my family and my friends. And he did. And I was so happy to think that we finally had a good, warm, and loving relationship. Until it didn't suit him or Joanne anymore. And he let me know that it really wasn't as good as I ever thought it was. But at least today I'm comfortable in most social and business settings and credit my current husband, Richard; my oma; the love of my friends and children; two good therapists; and that I had little choice but to bulldoze ahead if I was going to succeed and give my children a better life than I experienced.

∽

There was an incident after my father's first stroke when he had asked me to drive him to Aunt Jean and Uncle Jerry's house for lunch, something I was happy to do and had done previously. I had recently undergone a minor cosmetic procedure and knew it was not safe for me to drive as I was taking painkillers that made me a little loopy and disoriented, and I was in pain, as well. I told my father why I couldn't take him, but offered to arrange and pay for a cab (no Lyft or Uber then). He was very gracious and understanding, and we hung up. Joanne called moments later, shrieking, "I don't care if you just underwent a fucking liver transplant. Your father needs a ride and you need to take him." I explained my situation, but Joanne didn't care. Things started to get really bad after that incident. Joanne also accused me of "not caring about my dad and not ever doing anything for the family." I was very troubled and knew Joanne's deceitful campaign to break up the two of us had begun, again. And appallingly, but expectedly, my dad was all in.

∽

Thanksgivings were typically wonderful affairs at our house. There were usually more than twenty-four guests and, as before, the list always included Arthur and Joanne (when we were speaking). I had completely convinced myself that my father loved me and wanted to be with me. We had so much fun sharing Thanksgiving.

More than a few times, we flew my mother out to spend the long weekend with us. There was one Thanksgiving, however, that was especially painful and disturbing. Simon and his then wife, Danielle, and her parents, visiting from Paris and staying at their house, were thrilled to be part of the day. We flew my mother in, as well. We weren't getting along that well the day before, and it spilled into Thursday. I was cooking and we were still arguing a little, when out of nowhere, she started fuming, accusing me of "not being on her side" during the divorce (more than forty years before). She hollered at me, "You were very friendly with Anna who stole my husband, your father, when she lived with us. Also, your aunt Carol wasn't nice to me, and you liked her too."

I couldn't believe she actually said that. And why on Earth was she bringing this up now? Today? On Thanksgiving Day with a houseful of family and friends? I was despondent. Surprised. Stunned. I was twelve when my parents were divorced, and I was a mess. "What? Are you really serious? Anna was my cousin and I didn't know any better. I was a little girl. What are you talking about? And my aunt Carol? Who cares if I liked her? It had nothing to do with you." (Years later when my aunt Carol attended my mother's funeral, I ignored her and was somewhat hostile, recalling this incident. A few days after the funeral, while I was at the airport waiting for my flight home, I called her. She wasn't in, but I explained to my uncle Bob how sorry I was for my behavior and asked him to please have her call me back. She never did.)

My mother shot back angrily, "I just don't think you care about me as much as you should, Mia."

Mia McDaniel

"Damn you," I retorted. I wasn't proud of that line. It just came out of my mouth, without thinking.

Two hours later, after an alternately warm and icy Thanksgiving meal, my mother announced that she didn't want to stay at our house the next three evenings as had been planned but wanted to go home with Simon and Danielle and Danielle's family and stay with them. In their beautiful, but rather small two-bedroom home. And, she did. She left us and went home with Simon. She didn't call, and she didn't come back. We heard that she played cards and watched television with Danielle's parents and acted like "she didn't have a care in the world." Meanwhile, I had to try and explain to Sam and Michael why their oma wasn't coming back before flying home to Miami Beach (on the first-class ticket we bought her). And, I heard that Danielle's parents were also shocked by her behavior. That helped console me a little bit.

I couldn't understand why my parents were constantly finding something amiss with me. I had two wonderful children, and I was trying to make my marriage better. If Rob and I could fix our issues, we could have the family I always wanted. I was working from home as a publicist for a teaching hospital and a cancer hospital. I was arranging for publicity—interviews with local and national broadcast, and print media at the two hospitals for physicians, nurses, staff, and patients. During transplant surgery. During robotic surgery. And the latest technology. And using old technology in new ways. And in exam rooms, with physicians and television personalities with their massive egos, sucking all the air out of the room, trying to outdo each other's accomplishments.

I once arranged a news conference with two identical twin doctors performing a kidney transplant on two identical twin sisters. It ran with photographs in the Los Angeles Times and most of the local television stations produced a story. I watched a world-renowned physician, who developed the procedure for living donor lung transplants, perform the surgery on a young girl with cystic fibrosis, while a television crew was shooting the operation. I loved my career. One of my dearest producer friends Lorel, won an Emmy for a news story she did for me with the docs and a patient on a new treatment for breast cancer. It was more than a three-minute story on KNBC. That was a long time for a healthcare piece. My work was fulfilling and exciting. It became very challenging though in 1994 and 1995 when there was the famed Ford Bronco car chase with O. J. Simpson not far from our house. For a good part of that year and into the following year, local media (and most national outlets) did not want to cover anything but O.J.'s trial, especially when they were awaiting the jury's verdict. I was thrilled when it was finally over, and my press contacts were once again shooting stories with the doctors and patients at the hospitals I represented.

Most of my heartaches came from my parents, yet there were also times that I was very afraid that my marriage wasn't as stable as I thought. And it was very scary. But most often, it was my mother and father. I was just never good enough, no matter what I did for them. Or what I bought them. Or arranged for them. Or talked to them, like when my father was leaving Joanne. Or when Simon disappointed my father over something meaningless and he wanted my intervention. My father didn't even appreciate when I helped him with his depression.

When Ryan wasn't getting along with his mother, he just wanted to talk to me about it. I always talked to him, but also told him he should find a therapist. I would be happy to help him find one. He laughed, "That's ridiculous. They're only in it for the money. It would not only be a waste of my money, but my time as well."

Then my mother wanted to talk about leaving her third husband, Greg. Greg, a really sweet man, whom she met in the drunk tank when she was arrested for DUI. He became the man she adored more than any other. He was still stunned at her funeral (they'd been divorced for seven years) when more than a dozen people sought him out, including me and Simon, to tell him, "You were the true love of our mother's life. She loved you more than anyone she ever met, or married." At her funeral, Greg was not only sober for more than five years, but he was one of the committee chairs at his local Alcoholics Anonymous chapter.

Neither Simon nor I were invited to see our mother marry Greg, the groom who became our new stepfather, in 1981. Our parents had four weddings between them, after thirteen years to each other, and we weren't invited to any, other than when our father married Anna and our mother wouldn't allow us to attend.

But until my mother's death, the family soldiered on. We continued to have my father and Joanne over and fly my mother out from Florida. But then she got sick. She had emphysema. She needed me more than ever. To talk with her doctors. To help her financially. To come to Miami Beach as often as I could to make her feel better.

She continued to work a few more years, but after several hospitalizations, it got to be too much. And she relied on me more and more. Simon was wonderful with her each time she had a lengthy hospital stay, flying out to help, but otherwise he was too busy when she wanted her children to visit. My mother wanted us to visit constantly. I visited constantly. I took her to the specialty stores she couldn't afford for groceries; to electronics stores, for a new television; to linen/bath stores for sheets and towels. I thought that maybe if I bought my mother things that she wanted but couldn't afford, it might help. It didn't. She just asked for more.

There was one visit when I was feeling particularly vulnerable. Simon's wife Danielle had also flown in, and my mother was acting excessively kind and chummy with her, so much so that I began to feel very inferior. It appeared that the two of them were so close, and I was on the sidelines. And then I noticed the beautiful, blue and gold ring on Danielle's finger that looked like one of my mother's favorite costume rings. I asked Danielle about it, and she said that my mother had recently given it to her, along with some of her other favorite rings. I was surprised and agitated, not because she gave

Danielle a few rings, but because my mother knew how much I loved her rings, and she hadn't offered to give me any. She was obviously trying to show me how much she cared about her daughter-in-law. When Danielle left the room, I only half-jokingly asked her, "Do you love Danielle more than me? Are you fonder of her than you are of me?" She laughed and wouldn't answer. I felt like a foolish child and wished I hadn't asked.

Another incident that shook me was on my birthday in 2007. Danielle was with my mother again, and as the day progressed and my mother hadn't called me, I became increasingly worried that something was wrong. She typically called me very early in the morning every year. My first thought was that maybe Danielle had to take her to the hospital. I waited and waited until nearly 9:00 p.m. Eastern time and called her. She sounded fine. After a few minutes, I asked her why she hadn't called me. She asked me why I expected her to call me. I reminded her, in a very kind, nonconfrontational way that it was my birthday. She said she was sorry, but she forgot. Really? My mother forgot my birthday. I never brought it up again, but she did. Next time we spoke she claimed, "Every time we talk, you bring up that I forgot your birthday and I don't appreciate it." I let it go. I was embarrassed for her and so discouraged.

Mia McDaniel

Chapter 41

Mia & Rob & Arthur & Rose

I started therapy in my early forties—primarily because of my father, and to a lesser extent, my mother—at a time when many of my friends were also in therapy, but because of issues with their spouses or children or their careers. I was very insecure about myself, and it was directly relatable to the way my parents treated me. I finally began to understand that my near desperation to find a man to marry in college and after graduation was a replacement for what I never had as a daughter.

I started to grasp how my father treated me—telling me he loved me when it was just talk. All he cared about was himself. And then for a time, he appeared to be Anna's in every way. He didn't have time for me or my brother. Or my mother before she left him. I knew better than to ask him for anything. I took any little morsel he was willing to toss my way. A hug meant the world. A compliment on my professional life made me so happy. I pushed all the horrible things away and refused to believe he did what I somehow knew he did.

I had two different therapists over many years, and when I told each one about my childhood and got to the part about Anna, specifically that my father asked Anna to marry him, each therapist gasped, "He married her?" It reinforced everything I was learning about my promiscuous lifestyle in college and my neediness as a woman. My father was absent my entire life, even when he pretended not to be. And he did pretend not to be, for years.

My mother and father had little to no interest in their grandchildren, other than my mother hanging so many pictures on the walls for her friends to see. It was hurtful visiting her, knowing that the photographs were window dressing, not time spent enjoying Sam and Michael.

The one thing I always knew was that I wanted to be a mother. When you learn from your parents that you're not a priority, either you never want to be a parent or you desperately want to be one. I wanted my own family. I wanted kids who knew they would be loved. Cherished. I knew I would adore them. It would be the polar opposite of what I got from my father and mother. I knew I could be happy as a wife and mother more than anything else. I was blessed to also have a career that was fulfilling and that I loved. But while on my "husband search," I got my heart broken almost as much as my own father broke my heart. I wasn't able to see clearly what I was really doing.

I was frightened that Sam or even Michael would follow in my footsteps with the opposite sex when they were in college. I was afraid they would make the same bad decisions that I did. My parents made bad decisions and I made bad decisions. But my lack of judgment combined with such little self-worth made me so vulnerable and unaware during my college years. I knew I was going to have to change to become the kind of parent I had wanted and also wanted to eventually become. My therapist assured me that our children had a wonderful support system in me and their father, and it was highly unlikely it would ever be an issue for them.

Chapter 42

Sara

When we lived on Mulholland, my best friend was Sara. She was a wonderful woman who was very intimidating to me initially, with her long, beautiful nails, perfectly coiffed hair (although I always found it too short), and flawless makeup. She drove a fabulous, new car, had "a gazillion pairs of shoes," and was very involved in her kids' classrooms. She became a wonderful, loving, and caring "stand-in" for my father at family events when he was MIA, which was occurring more often.

I watched her as she willingly put herself out there to be an integral part of her kids' daily lives, interacting with parents and teachers, doing whatever she could to ensure their safety and their happiness. How I wished my mother would have been a little bit involved. Sara was a stellar mom, and I knew I wanted to be more involved and self-assured like she was. At first, I was far too intimidated by the parents and teachers when the kids were in elementary school. I was very self-conscious that I was an impostor. But Sara rubbed off on me, and I became much more involved in my kids' school. And Sara "talked me off the cliff" when my father frequently said something especially hurtful.

When Sara joined our family to see Sam's plays or Michael's baseball games, she was not the least bit intimidated by any celebrity. In fact, at one of Sam's plays when Tom Hanks said he didn't know how to be sure that his daughter got his bouquet when they took curtain calls, Sara was there to explain the process. She looked directly at him, and said, "It's easy. When they come out for curtain calls, you aim them right at her head and throw." Hanks and his wife broke up laughing. It was hilarious. She did this often, and we all loved her for it. And with Sara nearby, I was always more comfortable around celebrities and didn't constantly feel that I was embarrassing myself.

Once she flew first class, and the man sitting next to her looked very familiar. She asked, "Do I know you? Do you know me?" He told her he didn't think so. She asked if he was "a friend of Bill's," referring to Alcoholics Anonymous that she attended regularly since getting sober eight years earlier. He said he was, but that wasn't it. She couldn't figure it out. He finally told her, "I'm Bill Murray." His name didn't register.

She got up for a bottled water, and the flight attendant said, "Did you know you were sitting next to Bill Murray?" Sara said, "Okay." When walking back, his name suddenly clicked and she remembered who he was. She sped down the aisle, and shouted at him, "You didn't tell me you were Bill Murray, Bill Murray!"

My father liked Sara, and they often chatted with each other at our parties. He confided in her, like when he talked about our backyard. "I don't understand why they would buy a home with a slope and not a nice, level yard with a pool and a play area. I thought their kids meant the world to them," he obnoxiously said. When Sara told me about the conversation, I didn't reveal that I never knew that my father hated our wonderful "Capture the Flag" backyard. It was just another hurtful comment made by my clueless father.

In 2004, Michael was hit in the face with a baseball at one of his games and went down fast. I ran to him, along with two other fathers. When one tried to lift Michael, the other one said, "Don't lift him. I'm a doctor." The first father replied, "I'm lifting him. I'm a doctor too." It was so LA and so absurd. We went to the hospital and called Sara on the way. She was my "go-to," not my mother and father

Mia McDaniel

who were never there for me, even when we lived very close to one another. When Michael and I finally got home, Sara was there with ice, ice cream bars, and Advil. And lots of hugs and kisses. Rob and Sam were in New York, as Sam was interviewing for college.

When Sara's daughter, Katie, married her girlfriend Michelle, they had a stunning wedding in the California desert. Sam and Michael were in the wedding party and Sam's fiancé, Chris, and Richard and I were invited. It truly felt like we were all one family, and it was so sad that Sara had died three years before of a terminal lung disease.

Chapter 43
Sam & Michael & Mia & Rob

I'm proud and especially happy that both Sam and Michael loved their college experiences. The fear I harbored that my kids would have a miserable time socially in college did not come to fruition. Instead, they not only excelled academically, but joined various organizations (they both wrote for their college literary magazines, Michael was on an intramural baseball team, and Sam worked theater-related jobs) and made friends of both sexes, without compromising their values.

After college at The New School in New York City, Sam initially wanted to be an actor, which I found amazingly brave. I remember asking her when she was only six if she got scared in front of the camera. "It's a camera, Mom. What's there to be scared of?" she responded. She did her first commercial at six. She's now a writer and a voice-over talent and has written a book. She lives in Silver Lake with her fiancé. He's an actor and has written two books. They host an astrology podcast together.

Michael went to Syracuse University in upstate New York. It had a gorgeous, sprawling campus, the exact opposite of his sister's city campus. He had season tickets for basketball and football, and once a year, the family would fly up for a game. When I was in college, my mother and my oma made the six-hour drive to Gainesville. One time. My father, who was living in California, arranged a business trip to Florida so he could also see me. Once.

In 2007, my mother died. Sam was about to attend her graduation ceremony at The New School, and for Michael, it was in the middle of finals. Michael thought he wanted to be a sports agent, and he was studying that curriculum. I had a huge argument with his most prominent sports management professor. The professor told me, "I can't tell you how many times a student has told me his grandmother died. He cannot make up the final." Rob and I were very upset. I called the department head (and might have suggested I could get a Los Angeles Laker to speak at the school, as the father of one of Michael's best friends was their announcer. I had no shame). He said he would talk to the professor and not to worry. Michael took the final. He didn't do well because of his grandmother's death and decided sports management wasn't what he wanted to pursue. Instead, he majored in writing and rhetoric.

Just two weeks later, Rob, Nana, and I attended Sam's graduation, while Michael stayed in Syracuse. It was a beautiful, but bittersweet ceremony for me because of my mother's passing.

My mother's death was very traumatic. I didn't want Joanne to attend the funeral because she was so unkind to me. I desperately wanted her to stay away, and I told her so. True to form, my father was present at the funeral but wasn't there for me at all, and, of course, he flew to Miami Beach with Joanne. When Joanne and I had a heated discussion at the funeral reception in my mother's condo and Joanne stormed off, my father instantly took her side, without knowing what the conversation was about. I left moments after I got there, and no one in the family looked for me. I was missing at my mother's funeral reception.

∾

In 2001, Rob's advertising company went public. His shares went from a few thousand dollars to a nice, big nest egg. We could easily afford college for both of our children. Comfortable or not, I knew we would never make them cry if they asked for money for essential items.

Even though Rob worked very hard for the money he earned, this new financial freedom left me with a sense of guilt and obligation.

I needed to use this money to provide for my parents. So when I finally bought myself a new car, I not only bought my mother one as well, but also paid off my father's car.

For my mother, I spoke to an old friend who owned a car dealership in Miami Beach. He arranged for his general manager and one of his associates to drive to my mother's place of business with a giant red bow on the roof of a new car for her, along with his camera and plenty of film. Later they drove back to the dealership with her old car. Because I could never do enough for my parents, I also paid for my mother's car insurance for the rest of her life, among other bills. She was thrilled, of course. She made some phony pronouncement to me, "Just because you have some money, I didn't expect that you would spend it on me. I didn't think you needed to do that. It was very generous. Thank you." Nothing changed.

Within a few months, my mother needed or wanted something else. It was almost like the new car never happened. A few weeks after I surprised her with the car, I was so excited when my mother told me that the car I had given her was actually on her bucket list. I thought, "How great is that?" But then she added that it was in a different color.

Around this same time, Rob wanted to stop working. And, for the first time in his career, he wasn't giving it his all. He and the agency came to a mutual agreement that he would resign, with one year's salary, as he had been at the agency for twenty-three years, a tenure that was quite long in 2001. He wanted to continue his poetry on a grander level. He wanted to publish a book, which he eventually did. He also wanted his own office in our house, which would have been great, but we didn't have an extra room. He spent about eighteen months dominating the dining room with his computer, papers, pens, dirty dishes, glasses, and cords everywhere. And he didn't see the need to clean it up in the evenings. It was the source of many arguments. So he went in search of a small office near the beach to write.

Our marriage was not as good as it once was, and we were not getting along that well. We definitely had some rocky times in the past twenty-plus years, but this was worse. Now Rob was more excited about writing poetry than anything else. And I admit, I was not the perfect wife. In fact, he complained on more than one occasion, "I never expected you to work for yourself so much. I thought you'd work part-time, not more than forty-hour weeks. You rarely make dinner for us and that's not good for the kids either." He was right. I desperately needed to adjust my priorities.

He also needed to control his temper. He embarrassed me in front of friends and family and business associates when he blew up or drank too much. When we were invited to my current husband, Richard, and his then-wife Miri's annual holiday party, Rob drank so much wine that he stumbled out of the Peninsula Hotel restaurant and was very loud and obnoxious. I apologized to the couple the next day and knew I would never ask him to escort me again. Richard and Miri were shocked by his behavior.

There was also the time I hired a designer to create a website for my gift basket business, and Rob had an argument with him over something I wasn't privy to. I was stunned the next time I spoke with my designer when he said he wouldn't do business with me anymore if Rob was there.

The worst time was late one evening on the outside deck of our Mulholland home when he hollered at me extremely loudly because he had had far too much to drink. I had asked him if he would buy me an engagement ring. We had been married for seventeen years, and I still wore my oma's cubic zirconia engagement ring. When we first married, that was *exactly* the ring I wanted. But after seventeen years, I was sure he would agree to buy me a new one—"our own." He didn't. He railed at me, shouting, "You're a fucking princess. You want everything. I don't want to buy you a new ring." After a few minutes, one of the neighbors screamed, "Please, shut the fuck up."

He eventually relented but didn't want to go with me to pick it out. Sara came with me.

I told him numerous times that I was very worried about his drinking. There were a handful of times over our twenty-seven-year marriage when he blacked out after drinking too much and was hostile and mean and unreasonable. I told him that if he kept drinking, it was a deal breaker. Still, he kept drinking. I packed his bags and asked him to leave for a weekend because of his explosive behavior the night before. He left and stayed at a hotel.

We both knew we desperately needed couples therapy. We found someone who was referred by a trusted source, and we saw him weekly for months. We tried. It seemed to help a little but just not enough. It was getting much more difficult for the two of us to stay happy together.

It didn't help matters when the kids and I went to see his new office space. It was disconcerting, to say the least, at how absolutely stunning he'd made it. He hung shelves. He installed lighting, artwork, and things hanging from the ceiling. For nearly twenty years, he refused to pick up a hammer or screw in a light bulb, but he managed to create an amazing office for himself. I had no idea he was capable of accomplishing these tasks. On our first visit to his office, with my father and the kids in tow, I could hardly hide my dismay when I saw the incredible amount of work and love that went into designing his own space. Clearly, he was unwilling to do anything like that in his own home.

I was depressed, and we had a huge argument. It was about what it was so often about. He's writing poetry to the detriment of everything else, and I was argumentative and depressed and still not preparing dinner. Take-out was almost a nightly event. We were fighting and we were loud and he screamed at me that he didn't want to be around me, and he certainly wasn't interested in having sex with a woman who was loud and argumentative. "Go find someone else to sleep with," he shouted at me.

Mia McDaniel

I was shocked and so upset and desperate to be appreciated, I considered it. I was going to Miami Beach to see my mother, and Wendy was having a party. I stayed with my mother and called an old flame. We were both excited to see each other after so many years. We flirted and got together a few times for dinner and Starbucks. I was seriously considering having an affair with him. I was so unhappy. I wanted to. And he wanted to. One evening, we shared a long, sexy kiss. I knew I had to walk away. I wasn't going to leave my husband. And my old flame knew he was acting as my life preserver for the moment and there was nothing in it for him. We talked on the phone a couple of times after I returned to California, and I met him for coffee once when I was visiting my mother three months later. It was over and I would never, ever do anything like that again.

While there, I confided in my mother about what had happened and about my confusion and turmoil. I wanted her advice and guidance. It was the closest I had been to her in years because we were actually talking about me.

Months later, I discussed the whole debacle with my therapist and told her how my mother had encouraged the relationship and how talking about it brought us closer than ever before. It seemed to be a good thing, but in retrospect, it was foolish of me to seek her counsel at that time. I needed for her to try and discourage me, though I suspect I knew she wouldn't. But I do take full responsibility for the "almost affair."

Meanwhile, the rent on Rob's new office was draining, and we considered purchasing a larger house where he could have his own office. We started to look for a broker and, as had happened with every house we ever bought, (except for Mulholland because Rob's late best friend, George, was a real estate broker and negotiated the sale and gave us a deeply discounted price on his commission so we could afford the house) we went through more than one broker. The first one was found lacking, according to Rob. I remember the horrid cringe-worthy moment when we almost sold our second house, but the broker had made a big error. Because of this the family was not going to buy it. Rob turned purple, stared her in the face, and screamed, "You fucking incompetent bastard!" I was speechless and ashamed. I was later so grateful that this professional woman, who was actually quite good, was willing to continue working to sell the house. And a few months later, she did and obviously, wanted nothing to do with us ever again. Many years later, I saw her on the *Today* show doing an interview on real estate and I badly wanted to reach out to her and apologize, but I was still too embarrassed to contact her.

Chapter 44

Mia & Anna

In 2005, Anna and I got together for the first time in thirty-five years after I stumbled across the letter she had written me in the eighties. I was looking for a necklace she had given me that had recently come back in style—a large gold pendant with a sunflower and thick black lettering that said, "War is not healthy for children and other living things." I found it in an old jewelry box in the closet, carefully wrapped in tissue, placed on top of Anna's letter. I read her letter again and was overcome with sadness. What was I thinking? Was I that brainwashed by my parents that I was never going to speak with her again? The relationship I had with Anna for so many years was loving and warm, and yet I felt compelled to ignore her. Even as a grown woman.

I called her and left a voicemail. She responded a few hours later, and the first thing she said to me was, "Are you calling me because you want to get to know me again or because you want to know more about your childhood and your father?" I told her both, and she immediately apologized for saying what she said, afraid that the second part might have given me a bad impression.

We met for lunch a few weeks later at a restaurant in Calabasas, where she had been living for some time. I brought one of my grandmother's vintage, beaded handbags to gift her, and she was very touched. I was beyond thrilled to be able to give her something that meant so much to me. We lunched for nearly three hours. We both had a lot to say.

I learned that after my father left her, she was broken. She rented a house in North Hollywood with two old and trusted girlfriends and finally confided in someone, telling them, "He ran my life for the past fourteen years. But when he was ready to end it, he was pretty nasty. He knew he didn't have the control over me that he had when I was a child, a teen, and in my early twenties, so he let me know he was ready to move on and that was that. No going back. He abandoned me. He used me up and had no more use for me. He moved to Pittsburgh or Philadelphia or somewhere in Pennsylvania." Their collective jaws dropped. They didn't know the whole story until living with Anna for several months. She didn't discuss it with anyone who wasn't already aware of it. She told me several times over the years, "I couldn't share it. It was perverted and I was embarrassed."

It was so sad what my father had done to her. While I never truly believed she was "a vixen," I was so young (even when I wasn't) that I just didn't give it a whole lot of thought. I was supposed to forget her. My parents repeatedly drummed that into my head.

She was on her third marriage when we got together. Her second marriage had been in 1975 when she was twenty-nine, and she told me that "the only similarity to your father was that he wasn't especially thrilled when it was his time to be with his kids. At the time we met, his daughters were seven and three. They lived with their mother, and he didn't see them very often. That made me sad for them. And I worried about that because I really loved him and he loved me and I saw a man I could have a family with." She married Matt, who at thirty-one was a much better fit than being married to a man who was sixteen years her senior. She wanted a child and when dating Matt, he was all for it. However, when they were married, he wasn't so sure he wanted any more kids.

"Before the pregnancy, I was fighting depression. I thought I was truly on this earth to suffer, first with your father and now Matt." She told him she would leave him if he wouldn't have a child with her and so "he agreed to inseminate me." Her daughter Linda was born in 1981. "She was the best thing that ever happened to me, especially since I was so afraid nothing would go right for me after Arthur."

If Anna and I had been in touch back then, it would have been so exciting for me to know that she was able to find happiness after my abusive father left her. And it was only two years before I would be married and four years before I would have a child too. But I was still so influenced by my parents, who told me Anna was the reason for their divorce and who would have been crushed if I had gotten in touch with her. As much as I wanted to, I chose to remain in their good graces and not contact "the vixen." I thought about it for so long after we reunited. It was so painful to think about all the wasted years. All the years that were lost because my parents lied to me. I was too young and immature to understand that a child who was molested from the time she was twelve could in no way be held accountable for breaking up a marriage.

Anna told me that when Linda was nearly two, she was so excited to enroll in the Thousand Oaks Gymboree with her. (I remembered how excited I was when I took Sam and then Michael.) They went once weekly for just two weeks when she ran into my father with his new baby son. He was living in Northridge with Joanne and their son, Ryan, who was three years old, only one year older than Linda. Anna was thirty-seven. Arthur was fifty-three with his third child. "It was not easy. He said he wanted to be friends. But he honestly wanted more than that. He told me that I knew him better than anyone in his whole life, and it would be so good for him if we could start dating again and see where it took us." Dating again. Even though he was married to someone else. "It was irrelevant because I would have nothing to do with him, no matter what his situation was. I think I finally realized that his abandonment was the best thing to happen to me in a long time," she recalled.

Before she "read him a very small riot act," as she was not one to curse and scream and shout, she asked if he could please give her contact information for me and Simon. She thought about us all the time and was so sad that she never saw us. He wouldn't do it. She knew he wouldn't do it. "It was only logical that he wouldn't want me in touch with his grown children. It was a chasm of cover-up that he started when I was twelve. He would never give me the information to contact you. It was so, so sad. I cried for days." Before leaving, however, she calmly said to him, "Arthur, you're a gigantic asshole, and I don't want to be your friend or your girlfriend or your anything. Do not ever talk to me again. Go to hell. You always said you would burn there anyway."

Mia McDaniel

Chapter 45

Mia & Anna

In the summer of 2006, Anna and I went to Gladstones in Malibu, where we had been a few times when she was married to Arthur. We loved the restaurant and thought it would be good for us to go there again, just the two of us. It was wonderful being there but tough. Us reconnecting led to an unfortunate realization about my father and Anna's life during our time apart.

While Anna had survived my father, he was not the only man she had to overcome. She told me that around 1983, her second marriage started to unravel. "He was always kind of a 'Peter Pan' guy. Our friends called him that. He didn't want to grow up. He wasn't mature enough to be a grown man. And he was kind of a phony too. Matt did not have a good grip financially, and we always seemed to be struggling. It's probably why I gravitated toward him, being your father's opposite, in terms of money and maturity. I'm not sure I actually recognized that at the time though. It seems so crystal clear now," she told me.

In 1985, Matt left Anna for his secretary. What a fucking cliché. The secretary was also married at the time. "His secretary made it super difficult for me on purpose. She hated me because I was close to his parents. They loved me and I loved them. But she kept me away from them." Her relationship with her mother-in-law was over. And Matt married his third wife, Lila. Anna was fighting depression. Again. "Somehow I saved myself. It was long before I discovered therapy or medication. I had to be there for Linda."

It was 1988 when I first responded, rather cowardly, to the ten-page letter that Anna had sent me. I was still not ready to betray my parents, as I regrettably saw it then, but it was the day before Mother's Day, and in the letter, Anna said she had a child. I called her, but she was out. I asked the sitter to please tell Anna that Mia called to wish her a "Happy Mother's Day." Among the first things she said at our 2005 reunion was that that "was the most hopeful message of my life."

She then told me that my father often told her he "would burn in hell." She had revealed that when she described her accidental meeting with him at Gymboree, but I was rather shaken when she told me that he repeatedly expressed it. It showed a vulnerability and self-awareness that I never thought he had. Did he actually understand what it was to feel remorse?

I asked her why she thought he would say that and she said, "He knew. He knew that what he had done was wrong." He wouldn't elaborate, but she was certain that he meant by molesting her as a child and grooming her and chasing her for years and ignoring his wife and children. He knew it was shameful, disgraceful, and reprehensible. And he would pay in hell. It was one of the most surprising things I had ever heard about my father. Did he really have a conscience? If he did, he clearly ignored it for what he saw as a more worthy prize—Anna.

I was so happy to finally be back in touch with Anna and was sorry that so much time had gone by needlessly. My parents should never have tried to keep us apart. They didn't have to sanction it or like it, but they should never have tried to make me feel guilty. So many years wasted without someone who meant so much to me. I'm very grateful that she wanted to reunite after so many years had passed. I know we would all have been much happier and healthier if we could have stayed in touch. We truly loved each other unconditionally, and our lives are so enriched being together again.

Chapter 46

Rob & Mia

In August 2005, Rob was going to be sixty, and I wanted to celebrate this milestone in a big way, with an extravagant surprise birthday party for family and friends. And I wanted to invite relatives he hadn't seen in years: relatives on his father's side, as well as his mother's. To do this properly, I knew it would have to be in New York, and I knew it would have to be at Sardi's, one of our very favorite restaurants located in the heart of New York City's theater district. Famed for its 1,200 caricatures of famous people who have eaten there, the restaurant was established in 1927 by Vincent Sardi Sr. We dined there every chance we could: before or after every Broadway show, for lunch with Rob's mother and Aunt Jo, for dinner or drinks with friends, for family dinners every year. I spent nearly eight months planning and organizing his party.

I coordinated with Rob's aunt Jeannie who lived in the city and still had some ties with his late father's family, most of whom Rob hadn't been in touch with since after graduating college. She was happy to help and started making calls.

I coordinated with Nana to invite all the relatives on her side in New York and New Jersey. And, naturally, I invited my father and Joanne because I always needed him to be a part of my family. I paid for his airfare, their hotel, and car service to and from the airport. And I invited Simon and Danielle and many of our friends in Los Angeles and throughout the country. We had more than eighty guests.

I spoke with the catering manager weekly, if not more often, arranging the event, which included an Italian menu, featuring four entrees, a premium bar, a birthday cake, decorations, and entertainment, which included a pianist and a caricaturist (of course). I also hired a videographer. The party costs tens of thousands of dollars. And I couldn't have been more excited.

Aunt Jeannie gathered photos of Rob as a little boy, by himself and with his mom and dad and their relatives. I brought about a dozen photos of Rob, Sam, Michael, and me and placed all the photographs on easels or on the walls throughout the private dining room.

To keep it a big surprise, I arranged for the maître d' to seat us in a large table in the main dining room, assuming that Rob would think his mother and Aunt Jo would be surprising him and joining us. After some time passed, I was to come up with an excuse for us to go upstairs. Because I'm not particularly artful at any kind of subtlety, once the waiter served our drinks, I very clumsily announced that we needed to take the elevator upstairs. Sam and Michael looked at me like, "Really, now?" and Rob was just confused. I couldn't contain my excitement any longer.

I opened the giant double doors to the private room, and it nearly shook with "SURPRISE!" hollered by all our guests. Rob was stunned. The room was filled with cousins, aunts, and uncles he hadn't seen in more than thirty years, as well as relatives he saw last month. His dearest friends who still lived in the city were there, along with our friends from all over. He was so thrilled, and I thought he was really proud and pleased that I had spent so much time, energy, and love to celebrate his big day.

The pianist was the center of attention, as Rob's enormous Italian family were wonderful singers and entertained the room for hours with songs in Italian, along with classic tunes by Frank Sinatra, Dean Martin, and Tony Bennett. After dinner and cake and lots of celebrating, people began shouting, "Speech, Speech!"

Rob stepped up to the front of the room and stood by the massive piano. I took his hand, as he began to speak. At that moment, it seemed to me like he didn't really want to hold my hand. He was very emotional and talked about how excited he was to be the center of this amazing party. But I remember thinking that something was off. Was he overcome by emotion? Was something wrong or was I imagining things? It passed and I barely heard what he said, as I adoringly looked at him. It was a very good thing that I wasn't paying attention to what he said.

I was clearly in a party "afterglow." I was exhausted, in that wonderful way when you know you have "done good." I threw a fabulous party in an incredible venue in the most remarkable city for my husband of twenty-two years, at that time. It wasn't until the next day when Rob apologized to me for his speech that I knew our marriage was going to end. Maybe not next year, or the year after that, but it was doomed.

During Rob's speech, with me holding his hand and looking at him so lovingly, I didn't hear or didn't notice when he told the very attentive crowd, "There are two women in my life I am blessed to have known and shared most of my life with. Both of these beautiful women were with me for nearly every milestone, every happiness, every sadness, every birth, and every death. I would not be in such a tremendous place in my life today, with my children, my family, my friends, my career, my home, and its possessions if not for these women. I love you so much, Mom, and though she's not with us anymore, I love you too, Grandma. And thank you everyone for coming near and far to celebrate my sixtieth birthday."

Everyone shouted and clapped. I don't know if anyone noticed that Rob didn't even mention my name. I didn't hear it. I still felt radiant in my success as everyone congratulated me on "the best party we've ever been to."

When he apologized the next morning for not mentioning me in his speech and feebly thanked me for the party, I was literally in shock. I let it go and I think I said it was okay because I couldn't bear it. I couldn't process it, nor did I want to. He forgot that I was the most important woman in his life. Or at least one of the most important women. I never brought it up again, and I didn't ask any partygoers if they heard it. Not ever. But I knew I would never forget the shame I felt for him. Far more than I even felt for me.

Mia McDaniel

Chapter 47

Mia & Rob

The decision was made. We were looking for a bigger home. This was at a time when Michael was in college and Sam had just graduated. When sane people stayed where they were or downsized. But no. We wanted a bigger home. And we found one. The house was stunning. Five bedrooms, three of them en-suites, a powder room, and two bedrooms upstairs with a fifth bathroom, it was 3,700 square feet. It was mostly an open floor plan with an enormous living room and equally large family room, a completely renovated kitchen and breakfast nook, a pool and a hot tub. It also had a large, very private backyard with a slope going up to the house above. You could see backyards and side yards, but no homes in the back or on the sides of the house. It boasted a three-car garage and a gate enclosing the house with a big driveway that could nearly accommodate valet parking. It was an incredible house.

The fiasco started with a bad broker who searched in our current neighborhood, but it was far too expensive for a bigger house there, so we looked in Encino, one of the toniest communities in the San Fernando Valley and where Aunt Jean and Uncle Jerry had lived for many years. Our broker was not a particularly good negotiator, and we overpaid for the house. When we divorced and sold it four years later, the real estate market was tanking and we lost money. And for me, as gorgeous as the property was, it was a blessing to move. Rob and I weren't happy and hadn't been for a long time.

The best day in that house for me was the day we moved in. I remember loading my car with our chihuahua, Sir Mick, and our two cats and driving to the house, calling my mother along the way, arriving in front of the house, punching in the gate code (it was so fancy), unlocking the front door, and bringing in the beasts. It was sublime. It was awesome to watch the beasts look out the wall of windows in the living room and family room at the backyard, facing the pool, especially when ducks and their ducklings flew in and swam in the pool.

I had high hopes that the next best day would have been when I convinced my father to join me for lunch in our new house. I thought he would be proud that his daughter bought this beautiful new home, and I was still desperate to get his approval in my seemingly never-ending quest for it, even at fifty-three years old. I could barely sleep for two days because I was so excited that my daddy was coming to visit. Rob embarrassed me when he told me that I was being overly dramatic and that he was compelled to calm me down before my father arrived. I wasn't overly dramatic but very excited and nervous. My father was very cold the entire time, expressing no opinion whatsoever. What I thought would be a fond memory was actually pretty miserable, and I was so anxious for the afternoon to end.

I was not happy that Rob was still unwilling to help maintain the house. Even when the house was still in escrow and was inspected, Rob wanted no part of it. I tried to handle it, but it was like trying to read Greek or speak Chinese. I foolishly met with the former owner before we closed on the house, and he explained away any items the inspector found lacking. And then, salesman that he was, and with me way out of my element, I agreed to buy all of his patio furniture and three gigantic potted trees in the front yard that he convinced me absolutely had to go with the house. I always hated the trees, even when I planted flowers in the bottom of the pots to make them more appealing. And the patio furniture was crap that we tossed a month later.

I discussed my husband's lack of interest in our homes with my girlfriends, and they all said their husbands took care of the house and the yard (not the gardening, but making certain everything was in order and functioning properly). And the inspection prior to closing and the negotiating. Rob negotiated plenty at the advertising agency, being the executive in charge of buying commercial time on broadcast or print media. And he was good at it. My friends even told me about their husbands' "honey-do lists." I had never heard the term before. And I knew it would never be implemented at my house. I was on my own again, only this time with a huge house that needed regular maintenance, as all homes do. There was nothing fundamentally wrong with the house, but every time there was a minor problem, such as paint peeling off the front of the house, Rob complained, "We got ripped off on this big, expensive house. Nothing should go wrong with this house after how much we paid." I could never get him to see that shit happens, and you need to repair it. It had nothing to do with the property being neglected. It wasn't.

The backyard was beautiful with the pool, the hot tub, the pergola with a large built-in barbeque, and the more than seventy-five potted plants and flowers that I tended to nearly every day. I noticed that one of the drains in the cement was stopped up and water was pooling all around it. I went to Rob, admitting that the backyard was more my domain because of the plants, but I needed some help there. "Have you seen the drain outside? The one closest to the table and chairs? As you can see, it's not draining and that's not good. Can you please help me and get it fixed?"

"Mia, I haven't been in the backyard in six months. So, no. I haven't seen it," he retorted.

I was stunned and shouted, "What? What the fuck? You're a homeowner, of this big house and you're telling me that you haven't ventured into the backyard for six months? Not to look at anything? To see if something needs attention? Or just to admire the beauty?

Or the pool? Or my plants? Or just the gorgeous backyard? Are you fucking kidding me?"

He just didn't want to be bothered with anything. He wanted to write poetry and support the Catholic church he had joined a few years earlier. He was very involved with the church, assisting on "a pajama and sock drive" for an impoverished orphanage in Mexico and traveling on the bus a few times with fellow church members to the orphanage, where he lunched with the kids and played games. It took up a lot of his time. He wanted to go to Africa with his Catholic church. He asked me if I wanted to go with him, but he knew I likely wouldn't go on a Catholic retreat to another country. It was going to be "very Catholic," he admitted. But I urged him to go. It was a very good deed. And he was going on a separate, expensive, and luxurious safari with some of the group at the end of their good works. I was proud of him, but I couldn't understand why it was too difficult to participate in church activities and in the upkeep of our home. He truly expected me to take care of everything all of the time. It was always like that, and it didn't seem like it would ever change.

Then he had an opportunity to go with the church to Israel. Israel, the nation state of the Jewish people, where I had wanted to go my whole life. And he knew that. It was the only place in the world that I didn't want him to go to with the Catholic Church before we went together. And he knew that too. I wanted his first trip to Israel to be with me. And I wanted my first trip to be with him.

"Rob, you know I'm Jewish and have always wanted to go to Israel. Are you really considering going with your Church before you go with me?"

"You can come with us. There'll be a lot of touristy things, historical sites, and discussions. And some missionary work, though I think that's just for one or two days."

"Really? My first trip to Israel, the Jewish state, you expect me to go with your Catholic Church? And visit all the Catholic historical sites, like Bethlehem? And Nazareth?

Before I ever see The Wailing Wall? Or Yad Vashem? You can't be serious. How long have I talked about going there? I would have thought you wouldn't want that to be your first visit either when you know how much it means to me."

"So, you're saying I cannot go?"

"No, I'm saying that for me, you can go with your church to Paris, to Rome, to Bali, to Tokyo. Anywhere in the whole world but Israel."

"So you're not saying, 'Don't go?'"

"You're a big boy. I'm making it as clear as I can. Please reconsider."

A few days later, he went for his immunizations. I was stunned. I confronted him and when he said, "Yes, I'm absolutely going." I said, "This makes me so sad. Okay. Fine. I'm not going to take you to the airport or pick you up. I want a phone call when you land there and when you land back home."

He flew to Israel with fellow church members. He called me, as instructed. It wasn't the proverbial straw that broke the camel's back in the marriage, but it was a turning point. While he was gone, I replaced the dining room table and chairs that he insisted did not need to be replaced, even though they were more than twenty years old and showing signs of wear. I bought a new dining room hutch, a new family room sofa, some Tiffany lamps, and a few pairs of shoes, just because. When he came home, he didn't say a word other than, "Wow. It's all so beautiful." This was completely out of character for such an expensive purchase, a purchase that I would never have considered buying alone in all the years we were married. We always bought big-ticket items together. He never apologized for his trip. We never talked about it or the new furniture again.

A few years before Rob's church trip to Israel, Richard and Miri invited Rob and me to join them on an Israeli tour. For more than twenty years, their public relations/marketing firm created and implemented the marketing and public relations campaigns for the state of Israel. Each year, they arranged for a group of print journalists to tour with them for seven days across the small nation. Rob and

I were planning to join them, and I couldn't have been more excited. It would be a trip for our anniversary. Our twentieth anniversary. How fabulous. We had to pay our own way, for airfare and hotels, but most of the tourist attractions would be taken care of by the public relations firm.

About three months before the scheduled visit, the stock market was not doing well, and Rob got worried. Real worried. It was a scary time, but we still had the funds to go to Israel. Nevertheless, Rob made the decision that we could not spend the money to go. And since it was our anniversary, he decided we would return to Hawaii, where we spent our honeymoon. In actuality, the trip to Hawaii likely saved us a couple of thousand dollars at most. The trip wasn't bad. But it wasn't good. We argued. We dined out in a spectacular restaurant on the beach. We argued. We had spa appointments at the same time in different outdoor spaces that were private and gorgeous. When I took too much time to shower and dress after my massage, I found Rob a little ways away from the entrance and he was livid. "I hated every minute of that massage. It's not my idea of enjoyment. I'll never have one again. And I waited twenty minutes for you. What the fuck was that about?"

I was nearly speechless, but managed to say, "After that wonderful massage and pampering experience, you're hollering at me for keeping you waiting? You just ruined everything. I felt so good. So indulged. So special. You didn't like it? A drop-dead setting on the beach? A fabulous hour-long massage, and you're all pissed off?" I left him there and cried on the twelve-minute walk back to our room. He never apologized. He only said that he really didn't want to do it in the first place. It was so fucked up. We never attempted another spa day together.

Both our anniversary trip to Hawaii and Rob's trip to Israel happened when we lived in Encino, which was the darkest time in our marriage. We lived there for less than four years. We lost a lot of money on the house. We separated and divorced.

Mia McDaniel

I was very troubled more than a decade after my Hawaii trip with Rob, when I joined my new husband Richard on a business trip to Hawaii, to the Big Island. The hotel and the surrounding area looked so familiar, but I was sure I had never been there before. I just couldn't comprehend how it was all so recognizable.

I called Jane, a friend since the nineties, who had recommended the resort Rob and I stayed at ten years before. I wanted to talk about the enormous confusion I felt by the resorts' similarities, as I was certain Rob and I holidayed in Maui.

Jane has helped me through many crises in my marriage and professional life by knowing what to say when I had a meltdown. We became close friends and confidants and regularly scoffed at a mutual client who introduced us, telling me, "My dear friends Jane and Larry go to Cannes every year for the film festival because Larry is an entertainment lawyer. They're very impressive, and I just don't know if you and Jane will click. Try not to be intimidated by her."

Jane gently told me that Rob and I had stayed at that very place on the Big Island when we celebrated our twentieth anniversary. We were shocked that I had such an unhappy time on that trip that I didn't recall where we vacationed. We both found it very unsettling and deeply heart-wrenching.

Chapter 48

Anna & Bruce & Linda & Justin

In 2006, we invited Anna and Bruce to join us for one of my very favorite holidays: Thanksgiving.

I was particularly excited to meet Bruce, who Anna described as someone who couldn't have been less like my father or her second husband. He was the most decent man she had ever met. He was divorced with two grown children. And there was only one year between them. Bruce worked for the county as a landscaper and lived in Ventura, unlike her two previous husbands who were businessmen. He was kind and sweet, and they met at a "Singles without Partners" dance in Thousand Oaks. They started dating the following weekend when he asked her out, after calling, just like he said he would.

Anna told me that she told Bruce very early on, "I want to be married and cared for. This might sound old-fashioned, but I want to know what your intentions are." She said Bruce was thrilled to hear that because he was in love with her. Completely smitten. He wanted to get married in a year or two if they were still this happy—he expected they would be.

After two years together and still very much in love, Bruce and Anna got engaged and he moved into Anna and Linda's home. They married on Valentine's Day in 1998.

I was so excited that Anna finally had a partner who made her happy. She did confess though that there had been a problem. After about four years, they had some rough patches because she thought he was drinking too much. He wasn't nasty, but he did sometimes say hurtful things, things that always seem to creep out when some people have had too much to drink. She was scared and knew they had to do something to make their marriage work. He knew he had to stop drinking or he could lose her. They went to therapy for about nine months or so and separated. He moved out for four months. After therapy, they desperately wanted to be back together, and it's been working ever since.

Anna said, "He makes me feel so good about us and about myself. And that's not a feeling I've ever had before." And Linda is crazy about him and appreciated how he took such good care of her mother and how he took care of her, too, when she was younger. "She's very discerning about who she likes and who she doesn't. Now she's really attached to him." Her friends adore him and she's comfortable that other than the drinking problem that they resolved, he doesn't have issues. "He's a wonderful, kind, caring man who is a fantastic husband. I'd never experienced anything close to this before. I'm so grateful for this life," she told me.

Linda and her husband, Justin, have two children now and they call Anna, Grammy, and Bruce, Grandpa Bruce. There's no problem having three grandfathers, instead of two.

When the couple retired, the traveling began. They love cruises and have been on at least a dozen all over the world. Bruce said, "I never traveled like this before and every cruise was a fantastic adventure with Anna. We've been to the Caribbean, Alaska, and to Venice, Barcelona, and Athens. We feel like royalty on all our trips. We're so good together."

They've taken road trips to Yellowstone, the Grand Canyon, and Yosemite—which was especially wonderful as the last time she was there was with my father.

We saw each other often, as we were eager to make up for lost time. We became closer than ever talking about when we lived together and how we endured so much turmoil and heartbreak.

We couldn't see enough of each other. Anna and Bruce joined Rob and me and the kids at birthday parties, on Chanukah and Christmas, a Super Bowl party when Tom Petty and the Heartbreakers were the half-time band and Michael was at the game, and a *Mad Men* party, celebrating our favorite television series. And just to hang out.

The old man was once again out of the picture, so we were comfortable and happy to invite Anna and Bruce to join us whenever they could. My father and I hadn't been speaking since Joanne's unrelenting campaign to keep me out of my father's life began, excepting my digressions. In fact, one afternoon when I went to my father's apartment to visit him, Joanne wouldn't let me in. I started hollering through the open door, "Daddy, I'm out here, and Joanne won't let me in." He was in a wheelchair following his second stroke and couldn't physically do anything about it. But he could have told her off. He never lost his ability to speak, and I knew he could speak his mind if he wanted to. He'd hurt me for so many years with ugly remarks, even after both strokes. Yet he was silent.

Anna filled an emotional and physical void for me. She was family. It was wonderful. It was comforting to have my older sister finally join me and my family in our house. But I kept it a secret from my parents. I thought my mother and father would feel betrayed if they knew.

Unbeknownst to me, however, was that my father and mother knew of our reunion shortly after we saw each other for the first time. Apparently, Anna was so excited that she called a couple who were their best friends when they were married to each other and told them about us. They were thrilled for her and wanted to get my father's reaction. They called him and told him. He didn't know. The first thing he did was to call my mother. I found out because I randomly asked Anna if she was still in touch with the couple. She updated me and then mentioned that she told them about our reunion. I tried to hide my dismay, so as not to hurt her feelings, but I was definitely upset and she could tell. They told her that my mother said to my father, "I can't

Mia McDaniel

understand why Mia would want to be in touch with Anna after all these years. She was just her second cousin, not even a close relative." That disparaging remark demonstrated once again how unaware they were of what was important to me. That Anna was important to me. They had no compassion. They couldn't fathom that I would have been devastated at losing "my sister," and not just my second cousin, and that I would be thrilled to see her again. In retrospect, I shouldn't have been surprised.

Just as Michael was always there to help me through boyfriend, career, or parental issues, Richard was the friend that helped me get through so much trauma with my father, many years before we became romantically involved. He made himself available whenever I needed or wanted to talk. Whether he called me three hours later because of a client meeting, or at 11:00 p.m. at the end of a fundraising event, he knew how badly I needed to talk just by the sound of my voice, oftentimes crying, and he consistently helped and supported me. Richard has helped me in every conceivable way to be stronger and to lessen my parents' influence on me, particularly my father's.

Anna and Bruce, along with Linda and Justin, came to Encino one Friday night for a Sabbath dinner. Justin was Orthodox, and they were excited that I had invited Daniel Pearl's parents, Ruth and Judea, to bless the challah. (Daniel was an American journalist for *The Wall Street Journal* who was kidnapped and beheaded in Pakistan by al-Qaeda terrorists. His last words to his captors affirmed that his mother, his father, and he were Jewish. His parents created The Daniel Pearl Foundation, which promotes cross-cultural understanding through journalism, music, and innovative communications.) I had worked on a project for the foundation a few months prior when Richard retained them as a public relations client and I handled the press. The evening was very sweet, very somber, very loving.

My father and Joanne knew that I handled the press for the foundation because Simon had told them, and he let them know that it was a very special client for me and one that I did pro bono. I wanted them to know how much the Pearls meant to me, assuming that if they knew that, they would not take a personal interest in the organization, as once again, we weren't on good terms. I didn't want to have to worry about running into them at any of the Foundation's events.

When the Pearls debuted their film about their son, *A Mighty Heart*, starring Angelina Jolie, I took Anna with me to the screening/fundraiser. We were there for about twenty minutes when I saw my father and Joanne. I was shocked. There was no reason they should have been at the fundraiser since they had never expressed any interest in supporting the organization. Contrarily, when I wanted my father to attend the annual Los Angeles Holocaust Monument event, in which I handled the press for nearly twenty years, he showed up only once. I had asked him repeatedly to attend.

When I saw them, I panicked and asked Anna to walk away from me as quickly as she could. I was terrified of a scene if Anna and my father saw each other. Joanne came over and said hello. I said the same and couldn't walk away fast enough. I worried the rest of the evening that we would run into them again. I felt so defeated that they attended my event and so relieved when we left without any altercation.

Chapter 49
Mia & Sam

In April 2011, after Rob and I separated and sold our house in Encino, Sam and I rented a house in Bel Air. Michael was still working in the Bay area as a broadcaster. Their father had already moved to New York.

It was a beautiful, small three-bedroom home on a gorgeous street in the hills with a big backyard that I filled with potted flowers. There was an avocado tree that gave us the most delicious avocados we ever tasted. There was a chandelier in the living room from the 1800s that was spectacular and there was an enormous built-in bookcase in the little dining room. I loved arranging nearly all of my books in the floor-to-ceiling bookcase.

I did not have a housewarming party because I just didn't think Sam would like that. We did, however, entertain friends and family. We hosted Passover with dear friends and my cousin, Rusty joined us too. We hosted Thanksgiving and had a few small dinner parties. While it was a very difficult adjustment for both of us, Sam particularly struggled and was very unhappy about our divorce. I tried to talk with her about it, but she wasn't interested. That summer, Sam spent two weeks in New York with Rob and it seemed to help her accept the situation a little more.

Sam had a job in social media relations at a very fashionable, young clothing line, and for a few months, she really loved the job. Except for the commute. It was in downtown Los Angeles, meaning one hour minimum each way. She worked there for about a year and then started to pursue writing as a freelancer. She also penned a column in the first ever fashion magazine published in Beverly Hills.

After graduating from Syracuse, Michael convinced the Cape Cod Baseball League to hire him as a sports information officer (SIO). He desperately wanted to be a sportscaster, and he had the confidence that he could make the transition from SIO. After one year as an intern, he became the exclusive broadcaster for the league's Hyannis Harbor Hawks. His fifth and final summer with the league, he broadcast the annual all-star game on the local NPR affiliate, and Richard and I were there. His grandfather didn't even acknowledge his college graduation, or ask about the NPR broadcast.

I still had my public relations business, where I continued freelancing, and I had added two authors to my client roster. One of the authors, a psychologist, evolved into the Los Angeles media's "go-to guy" for stories on children and helping them understand their world during crises—be it personal, from commenting on how to handle your parent's divorce or bullying to events with national implications, including the horrible shooting at Sandy Hook in Connecticut that he was interviewed about on TODAY. And my very dear friend Pam wrote a cookbook dedicated to providing a healthier lifestyle by offering tested "anti-cancer recipes," after she recovered from the disease. I succeeded in getting press for Pam in Los Angeles, Sacramento, the Midwest, and cities across the country.

Mia McDaniel

Chapter 50
Richard

I met my current husband Richard in 1989, a few weeks before Michael lost his battle with AIDS. Richard was opening his marketing and public relations firm with Miri. He would handle the public relations and marketing and Miri handled their nonprofit fundraising division. It worked very well for more than twenty-two years.

Richard was "ahead of his time," as he wanted to hire a small amount of full-time employees and a bigger network of freelancers. He contacted a colleague who ran one of Los Angeles's largest public relations firms to see if he knew anyone who could handle media relations for his clients. He did. It was me, as I had been freelancing for the firm for almost three years.

Richard called me and inquired about my interest in working for his company as a freelancer. I was very interested. He invited me to his office the following week and asked me to bring my portfolio.

Oh no, I thought after I hung up. I was so bummed that he wanted to see a portfolio. I didn't have a portfolio. I'd been freelancing for nearly three years, for six major public relations firms in Los Angeles and New York, and they'd all been referrals. Nobody had ever asked me to show them a portfolio. Now I had to do a dog and pony show.

Not only did I have to create a portfolio, but I was also going to have to tell Richard that when he hired me, he hired "a team." While I specialized in media relations, talking with the press and persuading them to create stories on my clients, my dear friend and associate Carrie wrote all of my public relations materials, including press releases, media advisories, and pitch letters, and my clients loved her. We had been friends since 1984, when Carrie was my intern at an international public relations firm where we garnered press during the Olympics for my account, Fuji Photo Film, the official film of the 1984 Olympic Games. We went to some awesome Olympic events together. This was likely the most visible account of my career.

Richard and I lovingly called Carrie "a righteous Gentile." Not because she saved Jews from Nazis (she wasn't born until many, many years later) but because Richard and I, both Jews, worked every year for more than twenty years on arranging the annual Los Angeles Holocaust Monument event and getting as much press as possible (to never forget) for little or no pay. Carrie did all the writing at no charge for the yearly event (Yom Hashoah), the largest in California. Jane also covered it for the Jewish Journal in Los Angeles, where she freelanced and ended up teaching me so much about Judaism.

Jane, Carrie, and I had been close ever since we started working together and spent many hours on Zoom during the pandemic in 2020 and 2021. We have been to each other's baby showers, our children's birthday parties (Jane has four boys; Carrie, two boys), Bar Mitzvahs, celebrations at Mulholland and in Encino. And, in 2016, both friends came to my father's funeral, where they were a wonderful source of comfort during and after the miserable ceremony.

I created an impressive portfolio for Richard, the only client who ever asked to see it. Today, I still have the portfolio in the garage that I now share with Richard. Every few years, we look at it and laugh.

About two weeks after our first meeting, Richard tried repeatedly to reach me for a freelance gig. He called me nearly every day for a week, more than once, and was surprised and annoyed that I wasn't returning his calls. I finally called him back after about nine days at Rob's kind insistence.

"I'm sorry I haven't returned your calls. My best friend in the world died on November eighteenth."

Mia McDaniel

"Mia, I'm so sorry to hear that. You have my deepest condolences. May I ask what happened?"

"He died of AIDS. I don't know if you know anyone with the disease or know anyone who has died, but it seems that for now nobody wants to talk about it. He was my best friend ever."

"My partner and I have friends who are gay, and we've actually lost one friend. It's so terrible and again, I'm so sorry for what you're going through. I would very much like to work together, and maybe it would be good for you, but I completely understand if you would like me to try and find someone else."

"Can you give me until tomorrow to think about it? Please?"

"Of course. Tell me about your friend. If you want to," Richard replied.

I did. I told him all about Michael. All about the beginning, when I wouldn't believe he was gay. How he was the kindest, dearest, most loving man I'd ever known in a platonic way. We continued our conversation for almost two hours. A friendship blossomed.

The two of us worked together on the immediate project. I worked really hard, as I especially wanted to impress him after blowing him off for more than a week. The story wasn't an especially good one, but I was relentless and secured media to cover the news conference. I had a local network affiliate and a local newspaper. And, I had *TIME* magazine attend. *TIME* magazine was an outlet I had yet to score for one of my clients. The reporter came, took notes, and interviewed the client. But did not run a story. I was convinced that Michael facilitated his presence at the event. Richard was dazzled.

I was his freelance media director for more than twenty years before our relationship blossomed into a romantic one. Sometimes we worked together for weeks at a time. Sometimes we didn't speak for months. It just depended on the agency's needs. I was the only one Richard called to handle the press.

We worked on amazing organizations that helped abused, battered, and neglected children. We worked on a toy company.

We worked on the Daniel Pearl Foundation and on the Los Angeles Holocaust Monument that I initially didn't want anything to do with.

"Richard, I lost family in the Holocaust. I can't possibly work on this. It's too painful. Too weird."

"Mia, remember when we first started working together? You thought you couldn't do it because Michael had just died."

"Of course. That was different. I was grieving. This is too scary. It's too close to my family history."

"Think about it. You could do some enormous good, getting stories out there so nobody forgets. You're the best. You would also have a personal drive to do the spectacular work you always do."

"Okay. Okay. Thank you. Stop. I'll do it. You're right again. It will be very good for me. But I cannot take any payment for it. It would feel like dirty money to me."

"Thank you. Thank you. Come to the office at the end of the week, and we'll get started. I'm really grateful and happy that you've agreed to do this, Mia."

That was in 1992. We handled the Los Angeles Holocaust Monument until the builders decided to stop holding the ceremony in 2012. I had conflicts for only two of those years. And the one year that my father showed up, Richard, as the narrator, made a point of thanking me in his brief talk at the end of the ceremony, knowing that I would be so proud for my father to hear my name mentioned. I ran up to my father at the end of the ceremony, anxious to hear his reaction. I was going to ask him if we could go for coffee or a drink when I was finished and talk about it and let him know of all the press outlets I had arranged to cover the ceremony. He said he thought it was great but was in a hurry and had to leave. He stayed long enough to meet Richard, solely because he was standing next to me. I (foolishly) expected he would attend the event for years to come. That would be the only year he came. My Jewish father, who lost relatives in the Holocaust long before I was born, couldn't make time once a year to honor those who had died and the few who were still alive and present every year. And his daughter was handling the press.

Even after he and Joanne knew that I was deeply involved in arranging press for the annual ceremony, they managed to upset me when Yom Kippur came around. For two years, Rob, Sam, Michael, and I joined my father and Joanne at a temple he went to for Yom Kippur. Simon was there, too, though I didn't know that he had been joining them for about five years. This was the third time we were invited, and I honestly didn't know if anybody paid for the tickets or if we were just permitted to attend. I found out that third year when Joanne called me a few days before the services and told me I owed her $600 for our tickets. I was offended and just sad that my father was unwilling to pay for synagogue tickets for us, his children, and his grandchildren. I started to explain to Joanne that it wasn't about the money. We could pay for our tickets, but I was surprised and rather disturbed that he didn't want to pay for our tickets. We were his family. Why wasn't he happy that we were all going to commemorate the Jewish holidays together? She blew up, called me selfish and greedy, and yelled at me, "Don't you dare send me a check. We don't want it. Fine. You just think your dad and I should pay for everything." The last time my father paid for anything for me was college and that came with a gigantic price tag.

Richard was my biggest confidant. I would call him, sometimes in tears, to talk about my father. Richard was always there. Oftentimes he had to call me back (and I would say, "What, you have a better name on the other line?") It was hilarious when he said he did, "The Mayor of Los Angeles. I'll call you back."

For years, Richard suggested and then pleaded with me to tell my father he couldn't talk to me like that and that I should end our one-sided relationship. He was too toxic. This was the one time I didn't listen to Richard. My father continued to make my life miserable.

In 2011, my relationship with Richard changed. We hadn't spoken in some months and neither one of us was aware of the dramatic changes in each of our lives. In the fall of that year, we went on our first date. I invited him to a small, exclusive Tom Petty concert that was a fundraiser staged by a local radio station for the Los Angeles Mission, Tom's favorite local charity.

The Tom Petty concert near the end of 2011 was the turning point in my new life. Richard and I were inseparable after that. And we would live together when the Bel Air lease was up in April 2012, as we prepared to move to Sacramento. Sam and I, accompanied by Richard, scoured the city for "the perfect apartment" for Sam, as I was very nervous about her living alone for the first time since she was in college. We found a beautiful, large one-bedroom in Los Feliz, and I moved into Richard's Beverly Hills condo, with my three cats and dog.

I have been a devoted Tom Petty fan since I had the exciting opportunity to meet him at his Gainesville home in 1973. I knew guitarist Mike Campbell's roommate when I was a student at the University of Florida. It was one year before the band became Tom Petty and the Heartbreakers. Philip (the ex-roommate) and I saw a "private rehearsal" at Tom's house. It was magical. But, of course, I was far too insecure about everything—the way I looked, the way I spoke, the way I dealt with men, the way I looked at a potential rock star and his band. Who was I to tell the band whether or not I liked their music? It took me years to understand how very insecure and frightened I was of the world. Instead of just being a twenty-year-old college student who was excited to meet a local rock star, I was a little girl, afraid to meet him, thinking he would know that I wasn't worthy of meeting him. Remembering that day makes me feel sad, instead of happy and nostalgic. Whenever I told the story, I would say to my friends in jest that "I could have been Tom Petty's best friend." And just maybe, there's some truth to that if nearly everything didn't make me so unsure of myself and worried about what people would think of me. Not believing in myself was a direct result of the way my parents often spoke to me.

Mia McDaniel

Today, I have a signed guitar, given to me by Richard for my birthday in 2017, which was less than two months after Tom Petty died and less than three months after we last saw him in concert. I saw him six times. Twice with Sam at the Hollywood Bowl, and once with Sam when he performed with his first band, Mudcrutch, at the Troubadour in Hollywood. Rob didn't like him. We never saw Tom Petty together. We turned each other down when we weren't invested in the performer, rather than remembering our investment in each other.

So, asking Richard to a Tom Petty concert was quite the big deal. A very special event.

"Do you like Tom Petty?" I asked, after inviting him.

"I do," he exclaimed. He admitted months later that he was "pretty sure who he was and really did like the songs 'Don't Back Down' and 'Wildflowers.'"

Richard and I saw Tom Petty twice more in San Jose and Sacramento. Richard designed a Grammy reproduction that proclaims me as "The Ultimate Tom Petty Fan from 1974 to forever." I have blankets, mugs, travel bags, posters, a clock, and T-shirts. I also have a photograph of Tom Petty taken by a professional photographer at a Hollywood Bowl concert I attended, that ran in the *Los Angeles Times* the next day and a commissioned painting of the artist that Richard gave me for my birthday in Sacramento in 2014.

We had a wonderful time on our first date. We had dinner at a sushi place near the venue and saw a friend of mine at the concert. The two of us went for some wine after. We had so much history. We knew that our first date changed our lives.

Our first kiss, our first touch was magical. We had been friends for so long. We weren't worried that this new stage would ruin our friendship. We would move on to a romantic relationship and keep the friendship intact, just different. In 2012, we got engaged and married in 2013, almost twenty-five years after we met in 1989.

We moved to Sacramento because Richard was offered a phenomenal job opportunity. I couldn't have been happier to join him. I'd been in Los Angeles for thirty-five years, after spending eight in Miami Beach and Gainesville (University of Florida) and most of my childhood in New York and New Jersey. We were both feeling like LA was becoming more about smog, long commutes, over-crowded freeways, and unbelievably expensive homes (both of our last homes were about $2 million each and this was in the early 2000s) than about the joy of living in Los Angeles, that for both of us had been so good for so long. Richard, who had just turned sixty the month before we moved, was born and raised in Santa Monica. It was terribly difficult to leave Sam and Simon, but the flight was just over one hour and the drive about six hours. I knew I'd been a good mother. My children meant everything to me and always would, along with Richard. And while it was heartbreaking to leave my daughter, Sam was twenty-seven and I knew she would do well and we would see each other frequently. And Michael was working as a broadcaster at a college in the San Francisco Bay Area at the time, less than a two-hour commute to our Sacramento home.

It made me so happy that Simon lived only a few miles from Sam, who was living with her fiancé, Chris. Simon would always be there for Sam. His presence in Silver Lake was a blessing. I knew he and his girlfriend, Sophia (who became his wife in 2018) would visit us in Sacramento, and we would be going to Los Angeles several times a year.

We recently celebrated ten years in our home, with three cats and a mini goldendoodle, different beasts than when we moved in because a beloved cat and a beloved dog passed away. Each time I lose a pet, I get a tattoo. Richard and my friends are concerned that I will have tattoos all the way up to my thighs on both legs, in tribute to my animals, joining the three I currently have above my left ankle.

Mia McDaniel

Chapter 51

Mia & Richard

It wasn't until I started dating Richard, and subsequently married him in 2013, that I began to feel good about myself. My second husband. I have finally found my soulmate—not to be confused with Michael, my soulmate in a gorgeously platonic way for those twelve years that we knew each other before AIDS took his life. Richard is the man of my dreams.

For me, even my beloved Ben "couldn't hold a candle" to Richard. In fact, in 2016, Ben contacted me via Facebook, but I didn't respond. I was flattered, but I just wasn't interested enough to reply. Besides, I couldn't do that to Richard, even if he never found out.

Richard is the kindest, most generous, thoughtful, caring man I have ever known. And he is smart. And he is a very tall and handsome fashion plate. For twenty-five years he owned a public relations/marketing firm in Los Angeles. He has so many friends from college, from grade school, from the high-powered job he had before opening his own firm, and from the US Congress, where he worked right out of college. He adores Sam and Michael and they adore him. He is always there for them and they rely on him.

Chapter 52

Mia & Arthur & Simon

I spent so much of my adult life trying to have a good relationship with my father, and Simon was always there for me when I wanted help to try and make that happen. In 2009, when I asked Simon (again) to arrange for our dad to meet with the two of us in an attempt to help me shore up his love and affection, he was happy to. It would be the fourth time that I asked my little brother to try and bring my father and me together. The first time, Sam was nine months old, and I was so sad that my own father wouldn't meet his beautiful granddaughter. Simon arranged for us to meet for dinner in Pasadena. Simon joined us, as he always did. I brought my father a large can of Planters Salted Peanuts with a big bow on it, fondly remembering him loving them when I was a child. He was pleased. He brought me a velvet dress for Sam. Our relationship never lasted for too long.

For the 2009 reunion, Simon chose a small, sweet, outdoor coffee shop on Ventura Boulevard and Coldwater Canyon. It was a gorgeous day. Cool, but the sun was shining. Happy faces met at "the family summit." Simon and I went inside and got coffees and pastries and joined our dad on the outside terrace and we started talking. Simon was more like a moderator than a fellow conversant. Things were going okay. As usual, I was hopeful that my father would validate me. After about thirty minutes, he looked me directly in the eyes, with a very nasty face, and said, "I don't have to love all my children. And I dearly love my sons."

My heart was breaking and I could barely function, but I managed to keep it all inside and just said I had to go. I asked Simon to walk me to my car. I was sobbing when we got there and cried, "Why does he treat me like this? Why do he and Joanne hate me?"

Simon felt so bad for his big sister and shouted, "I don't know. I don't know. It's terrible. I'm sorry."

Joanne was largely to blame. The agony and criticism I endured when he was married to Joanne was far worse, almost incomparable, to his distaste for me when he was married to Anna. And far worse than when he was briefly unmarried, though he was rarely alone. Not only did Joanne have my father wrapped around her fingers and her toes, but she also wanted to destroy any relationship he had with me. She wanted to convince him that he didn't need his daughter. I was only in their way. They had their own child, their son. And they had Simon. I was unnecessary. "It's me or Mia," she made clear. He chose Joanne. And for a long time, he tried to pretend he hadn't.

I was either too naïve or just refused to accept that my father was manipulating me. That he had been manipulating me for years. After all, I paid the balance due (nearly $25,000) on his car in 2002, after Joanne's campaign began. I was effectively unaware of what my father and my second stepmother were capable of inflicting on me. Yet I didn't stop being there for him, even when it became glaringly obvious. But inevitably, I had to save myself and back off. It's sad though that it was well after he inflicted so much damage.

My brother and I came to understand that Joanne was the most calculating and disturbing person we had ever met. It was apparent that she knew when and how to blow up my relationship with my father. And, like Arthur, she was extremely intelligent. He bragged that she was a member of Mensa. Her intelligence was all she had. She had no empathy. She had no compassion for anyone, except their son, Ryan, and Arthur. And Simon, when it was beneficial to her. She was so confrontational, difficult, and exhausting.

At my father's funeral in 2016—which was dreadful, creepy, and unloving—my second husband approached Joanne, whom she had only met briefly once before. "Joanne," he said, "I'm Richard, Mia's husband. Nice job with the reception, but, I am appalled that you removed all the photos of Mia and of Arthur's grandchildren on the table in the corner. Mia went through so many pictures and brought about twenty photos of her, the kids, and her father, as Simon told us you asked, and we put them on that table when we arrived. But now they're all gone and only pictures of you, Ryan, Simon, and Arthur are there. None of him with his daughter and his grandchildren." Well, nobody ever speaks to Joanne like that. She quickly did an about-face and walked away. She went directly to Simon, so agitated that we thought she might explode, demanding to know why he "allowed" my husband to talk to her like that. Simon could barely speak. He was stunned. At Simon and Sophia's house that evening, Richard got high praise from the entire family. "Wow, Richard. Nice performance. You're awesome. You slayed the dragon."

A few weeks after Arthur's funeral, Simon was on the phone with Ryan. "When are we and your mother going to scatter our father's ashes? I know he wanted us to do so in Big Sur."

"My mother and I spread his ashes two weeks ago. She told me you had a conflict and couldn't join us."

"Thanks, Ryan. I didn't have any conflict. Your mother never called me."

It was very difficult for me to accept that my father was no longer part of my life during the last few years of his. I was "permitted" to go to the hospital only three times after his first stroke. When I walked in his room, I saw loving photos of my father, Joanne, Ryan, and Simon on the walls. The next time I came I brought photos of me and Rob and his grandchildren and added them to the collection. The last time I came around, all my photos were gone.

When he died, Simon was there and called us, "My father just died," he told Richard. I was four hundred miles away and so traumatized that things weren't different. That I wasn't part of the family. I wasn't allowed to be there when he died. I wasn't consulted on his funeral or the spreading of his ashes. I had done nothing to deserve that isolation. He did nothing to change it, long before strokes altered his behavior.

Chapter 53
Mia & Richard

It was serendipitous when, in January of 2012, Richard spoke with a dear friend of thirty-five years who lived in Sacramento. Richard wanted his public relations/marketing firm to represent the enormous California state-run organization in which his friend was now the director. A meeting was scheduled in Sacramento, and Richard and I met with Bob and his wife, Tara. We had a wonderful dinner at a local restaurant with plenty of good wine (Bob and Tara bottled their own label), and as Richard was about to make his pitch, Bob said to him, "I need a sales and marketing head of my organization. I want you to fill it!" I was so excited to hear this I shouted, "He'll take it!"

We talked for the next two hours, and when we got to our hotel, I began sobbing. "What have I done? I can't leave Los Angeles and Sam. What was I thinking?" Richard calmed me down, as he had successfully done so many times over the years (primarily about my father) and we would continue the discussion when we got back to LA. Richard and Bob would meet a few more times in Northern California.

After a few months and much discussion, the two of us decided it would be a wonderful move professionally and a fantastic place to relocate to and we started the process. As the position required an appointment by Governor Jerry Brown, we had to wait as Richard went through the process. Finally, in February of 2012, we went to Sacramento for Richard's final interview and waited some more. In March it became official. Richard got the job as Bob's director of sales and marketing. We made a few trips to Sacramento to find a house and moved into a home we adore on May 25, 2012.

Our new home was flipped a few months before our broker showed it to us. It was nearly everything we wanted. Three bedrooms, three baths (so Sam and Chris and Michael could visit at the same time), a completely open format with a spacious living room, dining room, and family room. Also, a pool in the backyard and a pretty front yard that would later be landscaped by Richard's niece. We've made significant home renovations every few years and we love the neighborhood.

My biggest fear in moving north, besides being six hours away from our families, was that I wouldn't make friends. So many of my friends in Los Angeles were made through my kid's schools. Parents became friends once kids became friends. The kids were grown. Who would I meet?

Our neighborhood is the polar opposite of Southern California. In fact, we had spent just one night in the house when our neighbors knocked on the door and invited us for dinner that weekend. And two days after that, I saw four women chatting at the home across the street from ours. I joined the conversation and was stunned that they were all neighbors and knew one another. In Los Angeles, I barely knew my neighbors. It was more of a "hello" in the morning, as neighbors drove out of their garages and a "good night" in the evening when everyone came home. Here were four women who all lived on two blocks and hung out together. It was almost unbelievable. And they have become some of my dearest, most treasured friends in the world.

All of my newest friends had big shoulders for me to cry on when my father died. They were all there for me with words of comfort. And soup.

How did this happen? I feel so blessed. I get from my new friends, along with all of my old friends and my husband and children, all the love and support that was totally absent from my mother and father during most of my childhood and adolescence. And when I was a young adult. And newly married. And when I had one child. And with two children. Today, I'm comfortable asking any one of my new friends for nearly anything. And they know it's mutual.

Chapter 54

Mia & Richard & Arthur & Joanne

In 2015, while living in Sacramento, my cousin Rusty's son, Cliff, was getting married, and Richard and I and Sam and Chris (who became very close to the couple) and Michael were, of course, invited. And my father and Joanne were going to be there. It was especially important to Rusty that I attend the wedding. Not so much to celebrate his son's marriage, but because he fantasized that a loving reunion with me and my dad would take place at Cliff's wedding.

In fact, Rusty said to me a few years earlier, "Why aren't you talking to your father? I see him pretty often, and I just don't understand why you don't care about him more and why you don't visit him and call him."

"Rusty, my relationship with my father has been torturous for many years. He's not who you think he is and who you would like him to be."

"So what? If you don't fix your relationship with him, I can't speak to you anymore."

"But my relationship with my father has nothing to do with you. We're cousins. We have a great connection and have for so many years. You'll throw that away because I'm not talking to my father?"

"Yes. I will." And he did. He refused to speak with me again. I was astounded. And very hurt, but he had made up his mind. Now, I was going to see my father and Joanne *and* Rusty at the wedding.

We arrived at the wedding and headed toward the martini bar. After one drink, I told Richard and Simon I was ready to say hi to my father. He was in his wheelchair, having suffered his second stroke years before. But wheelchair or not, he was the same man as he was my whole life. He wasn't a sick, pathetic stroke victim in a wheelchair. He was my father, who could still hurt me. He hadn't lost his communication skills. He could still speak relatively articulately and he could show his emotions with one look of disapproval on his face. He actually looked handsome in his dark suit and tie. Exactly like he used to look, only in a wheelchair now.

As soon as I saw my father, I was twelve again. And Rusty watched as Richard and I approached him. Richard, always protecting me, started the conversation, "Arthur, I'm Richard, your daughter's husband and I love her more than anything in the world and will always take care of her." My father looked at him like he was an alien and didn't say a word.

Then it was my turn. "Hi, Daddy. It's good to see you here. Let's take some pictures of us together." And Simon took his cell phone out of his pocket, as I directed the shoot with me on one side of my father and Richard on the other. "Daddy, I'm going to come in for a kiss and Simon will take a photo." I put my face up against his, and he started to smile for two photos. Then he saw Joanne and his smile faded. He just sat there, as if he was being physically forced against his will to appear in a photograph with his daughter. Rusty witnessed it all, but he didn't see it. He appeared thrilled, as if the two of us had become close again. Or maybe close for the first time. It was so depressing.

Cliff's wedding brought back terrible memories of Rusty's wedding in 1982, when I was not allowed to speak with my father because of his "just pretend I'm dead" pronouncement. The wedding was at the couple's new home in Pacific Palisades, with champagne and hors d'oeuvres beautifully spread out in the living room and on their back patio. Whenever Rob and I were in the living room, we saw my father and Joanne on the patio. When on the patio, my father and Joanne were in the living room. It was the first time Rob had ever seen my father and it was dreadful. We left as early as we could without an explanation. And once again, I saw my father and left him, sobbing. I was so sad. At Rusty's wedding, he couldn't even be civil or kind or a father.

For Cliff's wedding, my father and I hadn't seen each other since a few days before his eightieth birthday (almost six years prior), when Joanne threw him a big party at his favorite restaurant. Rusty and his date were there. Scott was there. Simon and Sophia were there. Simon's ex-wife, Danielle, and her boyfriend were there. The few friends the couple had were there. Rob, Sam, Michael, and I were not invited. Just days earlier, I had treated my father to a manicure and pedicure at a salon I took him to every few months, followed by conversation over coffee and pastries at Starbucks. That weekend was his birthday. But I was afraid to ask if we were invited. I didn't want a confrontation with him and figured we must be invited after all we'd done for him and because we were his family. Even though I unquestionably knew better, it was only four days away and we hadn't received an invitation (I heard there were mailed invitations).

Even after it was crystal clear that the four of us were not invited, I showered him with birthday presents, carefully and beautifully wrapping the gifts in gorgeous paper and giant ribbons. I gave them to Sophia to give to my father. Three special gifts that I knew he would love: a gorgeous Frank Lloyd Wright stained glass window (he idolized the architect), a paperweight of crinkled blueprints (as a child, I once "surprised" my parents by cleaning the basement, crinkling and throwing away his blueprints, when he was still an architect), and Frank Sinatra's latest *Duets* CD, (his very favorite singer). Why? Because I was always on a campaign to get his love, to get his approval, to get him to pay attention to me, even when I was in my fifties and he made it clear he had no interest. It never ended. I'm embarrassed and sad when I think about the love and care that went into the selection and wrapping of his gifts.

In spite of my father's cheating and abuse and insults, I managed to keep my dignity and foster the best relationship with Simon.

We were both so troubled as kids and young adults and there were times when we weren't comfortable around each other. In retrospect, I see the discomfort as a result of both parents playing mind games with us for years. Destroying our self-confidence rather than helping us build it up. Simon tells me today, "You took a bullet for me because you were older. And I truly didn't appreciate that until I was nearly forty." We both wish we had been able to speak about the incredibly dysfunctional family situation we endured when we were very young. But we always managed to be close, and Simon consistently told me that I was a wonderful protector of my little brother.

The day after the party, my father called me. He got the presents, "Thanks. But you couldn't call me on my birthday?" I felt like I had been broken, and once again, he broke me. I shouldn't have been surprised. When I was in high school, I was excited to call him for his birthday during a break between classes. I only had a few minutes, so I ran to the payphone and called him in Southern California collect. I wanted to know if he liked the gifts I had sent. He accepted the call and after I sang "Happy Birthday," he hollered at me for calling collect. I was crushed.

The call he made to me after his eightieth birthday was the last time we spoke until Cliff's wedding, though he repeatedly called and left voicemails asking for money. Money he felt entitled to. "I'm your father. I want some money and I understand you have some. You owe me that." I had always been very generous with my father, giving him anything he may need and making sure he was more than taken care of, yet it never seemed to be enough for him. He continued to leave me voicemails with him hollering as opposed to speaking. At one point, I was so depressed, I considered sending him $10,000 to get him to either leave me alone or to try and buy his love again. I couldn't recall which it was that time, though I suspect it was the latter. God bless Richard for talking me out of it. It would have undoubtedly only led to more calls, more heartbreak. He was dead five months later.

Chapter 55
Mia & Richard

Richard and I got married in June 2013 in the State Capitol by former California Attorney General and then current State Treasurer Bill Lockyer (who Richard befriended and asked if he would do us the honor). In October we hosted our wedding party in our backyard with nearly seventy-five friends and family. It was very special for me to share my day with Anna, as between the two of us, five marriages were held and three children were born and this was the first life event we could celebrate together since I was fourteen.

Along with Anna, our closest family and friends joined us, including friends I made years ago—from Miami Beach, Manhattan Beach, New York, Encino, and Los Angeles. Friends I've known for forty years and friends I'd known less than one year in our new home.

"It was a gorgeous party in our backyard. We had the pool covered by a company that specializes in that sort of thing and we had a DJ playing a lot of Tom Petty. And we had a dance floor. And twinkle lights everywhere and market lights strung across the pool that was now covered with eight tables and four more tables in the yard. We had two chefs set up in the garage preparing filet mignon and salmon. And the bar was stocked with everything anyone could possibly want, along with champagne toasts. And a giant table with fabulous desserts and a gorgeous wedding cake. And there was an intimate little table for smoking cigars at the end of the evening. And the most special was having Simon and his dear musician friend Jimmy sing and play guitar for us during cocktails, before dinner.

The live music was truly one of the most wonderful gifts we received. And our wonderful friends, some for more than forty years, traveling across the country to join us for our wedding party. Friends who had been with me over the years and particularly, with Mia, during enormously troubled and confusing times," Richard recalled.

"I was thrilled with everything that night. Not only were the kids, Sam and Chris and Michael there, along with treasured friends, but Anna was there. And she was happy now, too, with Bruce. After so many years separated, Anna and Mia reunited and celebrated together. After so much trauma endured by the two women, they came together, and their relationship was stronger than ever before. I was thrilled to witness it and to be such an integral part of it," he added.

Mia McDaniel

Epilogue

In June of 2022, Richard and I celebrated nine years of marriage. While we are both profoundly happy, I feel especially blessed that I have thrived in this marriage. I'm responsible for my adult life, not my parents. But it was discouraging growing up in a household where there was so little love and support from them. They didn't "have my back"; they were terrible role models; and they never put me and my brother first. And they lied. My father blew up his family without one bit of regard for his wife or his children. Or for Anna, the young girl whose life he nearly ruined.

Yet, there were times when I felt foolishly proud of him because he was smart. Because he wouldn't give up on college, even when it took him eleven years to graduate. Because he was "hip." We smoked weed at his home with Anna when it was illegal. He was handsome and charming when he chose to turn it on. He kept leaving me and I kept doing everything possible to convince him to come back to me and love me. I hoped it would be enough that he came back. Again and again. At my urging.

But it wasn't enough. Neither one of my parents taught us life lessons. Taught us how to grow up. Taught us how to love. My father's legacy is a horrible one comprised of his abuse, absence in his children's lives, and a terrible case of narcissism and selfishness with a critical lack of caring for anyone but himself. He was a good actor. It took me years to recognize that. And my mother provided no counterbalance to him. In fact, her behavior and many of her judgmental comments had significant negative impacts on me.

I struggled needlessly, questioning everything I thought I knew about myself because of her condescending opinions. So many times, it felt like she took away permission for me to believe in myself. If not for my oma, I'm not sure I would know how to love. My heart grew in spite of my parents, not because of them.

The journey that brought me to realize how negative and trying it was for me to survive, let alone thrive, with Arthur as my father, has finally given me peace. Peace to understand that I am good, and I should not carry guilt for the painful feelings I hold regarding my parents today. Also, I have let go of most of my shame for acting out in college and in my early twenties. I regret my bad decisions, but I'm no longer paralyzed by them.

Finally, I admit that my father was a pedophile. But, I have to add the caveat, only with Anna (which I understand is fairly irrelevant). And no matter how many times my parents tried to get me to believe that I was failing them, I know otherwise. Now, at sixty-eight.

The journey I took with Anna has been one of self-realization for both of us, and we have broken the cycle so the next generation will not be impacted in the same way we were.

Because children have a much greater chance of loving and living fulfilling lives if their parents are there for them growing up, and as adults, Richard and I always have Sam and Michael's back. And Anna and Bruce always have Linda and their grandchildren's. Now we are always there for each other. The two "sisters/cousins."

Nearly three years after my father's death, Simon called me to tell me about a session he had with a medium who communicated with the spirit world. Simon had no agenda when he set up the meeting and the medium had no agenda either. Simon said she knew nothing about his life or his family. Didn't know he had a sister. Didn't know his father had died.

Right away, she told him that she was in touch with his father and saw him wildly sobbing. Heartbreakingly crying out that it was too late to change the way he had treated his daughter. He couldn't repair their relationship. Not anymore because he was dead and burning in Hell. Just like he expected he would be.

Acknowledgments

My gratitude and sincere thanks to my dear friends Pam Braun, Jane Ulman, and our recently adopted daughter, Ryann Petite-Frere, who graciously read my drafts and couldn't have helped me more in pursuit of this dream! And my darling Richard, who listened to me cry and holler and complain for nearly three years and never wavered. And to my cherished Michael and Samantha and her husband Chris.

And to beloved friends and family, including my brother, Simon Weinberg and his wife, Sophia, Anita Bartman Edman, Kathi Klingler, Chris Loeb, Linsey Degen Sandberg, Soonhee Hong, Charmaine Morrison, Virginia Rich, Liz Ghettys, and Evelyn Jensen.

And much appreciation and heartfelt thanks to some of my biggest supporters, including Carrie St. Michel, Marianne Moloney and Dr. Carol Tannenbaum for unfaltering encouragement and believing in me.

And to Anna, for spending hours with me, telling me the truth, which was frequently extremely difficult for her to express and for me to learn. And her husband, Bruce for supporting her when it became tougher than we all expected.

To Hailie Johnson—I often wondered how sincere it was when authors thanked their editors and now I understand. And to Tyson Cornell, who said my memoir was compelling and he wanted to publish it and worked closely with me along the way.